AF632946

PILGRIMAGE TO KAILASH

The Indian Route

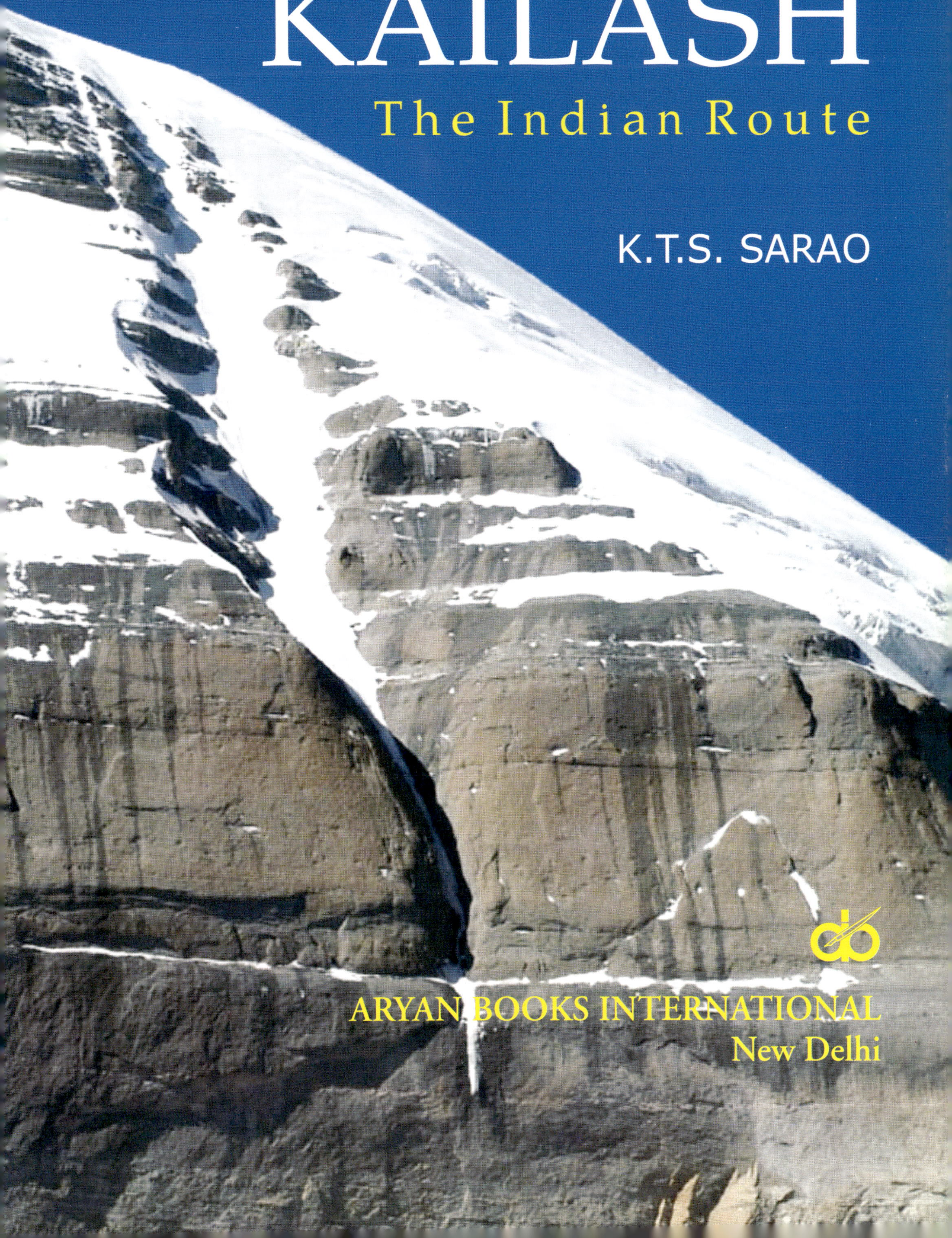

PILGRIMAGE TO KAILASH

The Indian Route

K.T.S. SARAO

ARYAN BOOKS INTERNATIONAL
New Delhi

PILGRIMAGE TO KAILASH
The Indian Route

ISBN: 978-81-7305-368-9

© **Author, 2009**

The publication of this book has been made possible by financial support received through the ASIHSS Grant of the UGC.

All rights reserved. No part of this publication may be reproduced, or transmitted in any form or by any means, electronic or mechanical, including photocopying, recording or by any information storage and retrieval system, without permission in writing from the publisher.

Published in **2009** by:

ARYAN BOOKS INTERNATIONAL
Pooja Apartments, 4B, Ansari Road, Darya Ganj, New Delhi - 110 002 (India)
Tel.: 23287589, 23255799; Fax: 91-11-23270385
E-mail: aryanbooks@vsnl.com, aryanbooks@gmail.com

Computer Typeset and Printed in India at
ABI Prints and Publishing Co., New Delhi

THIS BOOK IS DEDICATED TO MY FRIENDS

Malay Kumar Sinha
and
Sudhir Pratap Singh

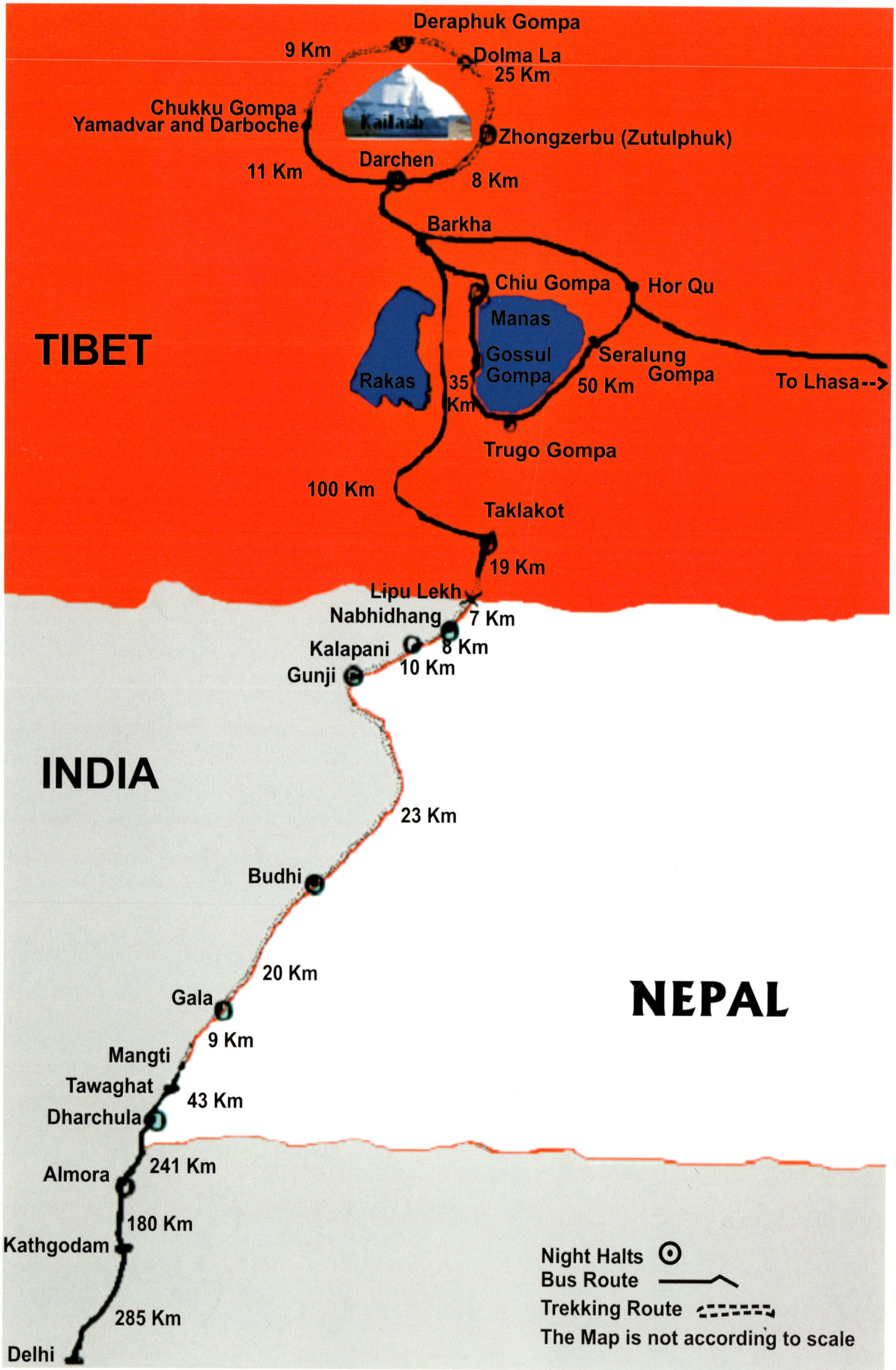

Indian Route of the Kailash-Manasarovar Yatra.

Contents

KAILASH PARIKRAMĀ AND OTHER ROUTES

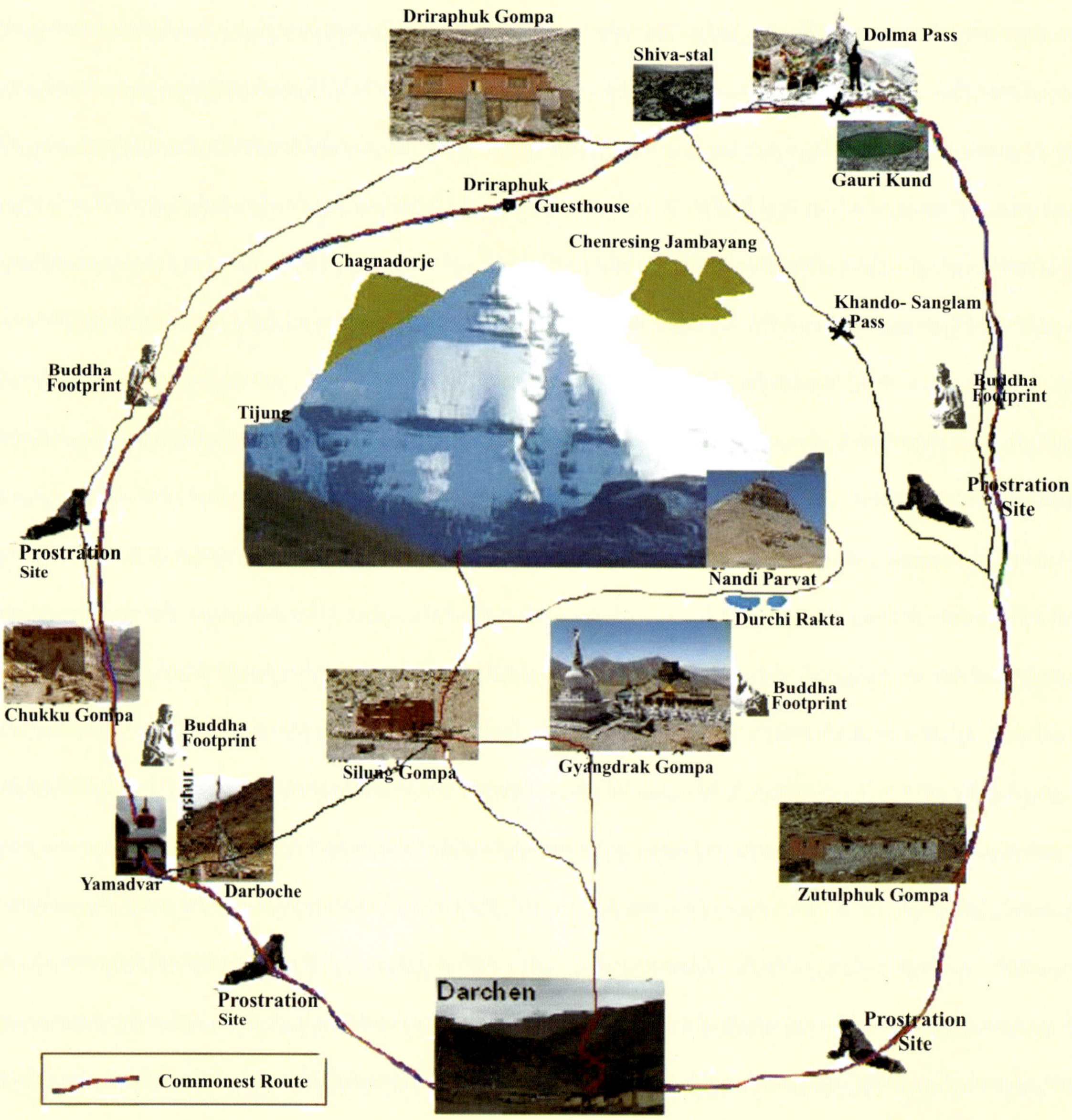

Preface

The Lipu Lekh crossing was reopened in 1981 for Indian pilgrims after a gap of over two decades. Though I was lucky to be chosen by the Indian Government to visit Kailash and Manasarovar in 1981 but due to financial constraints I could not make it. Finally, an opportunity came my way when my friend Sudhir Pratap Singh was chosen as the Liaison Officer of the thirteenth batch in the Kumbh year of 2002. By now my financial situation had also somewhat improved. Then in 2004 my friend Malay Kumar Sinha helped me to successfully visit the Kailash region by untangling the various bureaucratic skeins for me. It would have been impossible for me to perform these two journeys without the help of Sudhir and Malay. Thus, I have dedicated this book to them both. After the visits of 2002 and 2004, I have been lucky to visit the Kailash region a couple of times more. In the year 2005, I went there with my friends Anita Sharma and Surinder Kumar and their son Manik. This trip was via the Kodari-Niyalam-Saga- Prayang-Hore Qu route. Then in 2006 I had the opportunity to go with ten of my students and colleagues to Adi-Kailash and Om Parvat. During the summer of 2008, I was appointed the Liaison Officer of the first batch by the Ministry of External Affairs (Govt. of India) to lead the pilgrims to Kailash. However, the Chinese Government refused to allow this and the following two batches to enter China.

This book has been prepared keeping in mind both the general reader and the specialist. As a result, attention has been paid to all those minor details which a general pilgrim should know. Useful information on the various spots which fall on the pilgrimage route, flora and fauna, and socio-religious life of the people, has also been included. Popular versions of the modern names have been used and as far as possible, diacritical marks etc. have been kept to the bare minimum. Thus, instead of 'Kailāsa/Kailāśa' and 'Mānasarovara', I have used the popular spellings such as 'Kailash' and 'Manasarovar'. Dr. Kalsang Wangmo helped with the correct spellings of Tibetan terms.

Apart from the above stated persons, Sunita, Jarnail, Anu, Neha, Nidhi, Kanika, and Kanishk have contributed in various ways towards the completion of this book. Last but not the least, I am grateful to Shri Vikas Arya of Aryan Books Interantional for taking keen interest in the publication of this book.

August 2008 **K.T.S. Sarao**

MĀNASAROVAR PARIKRAMĀ

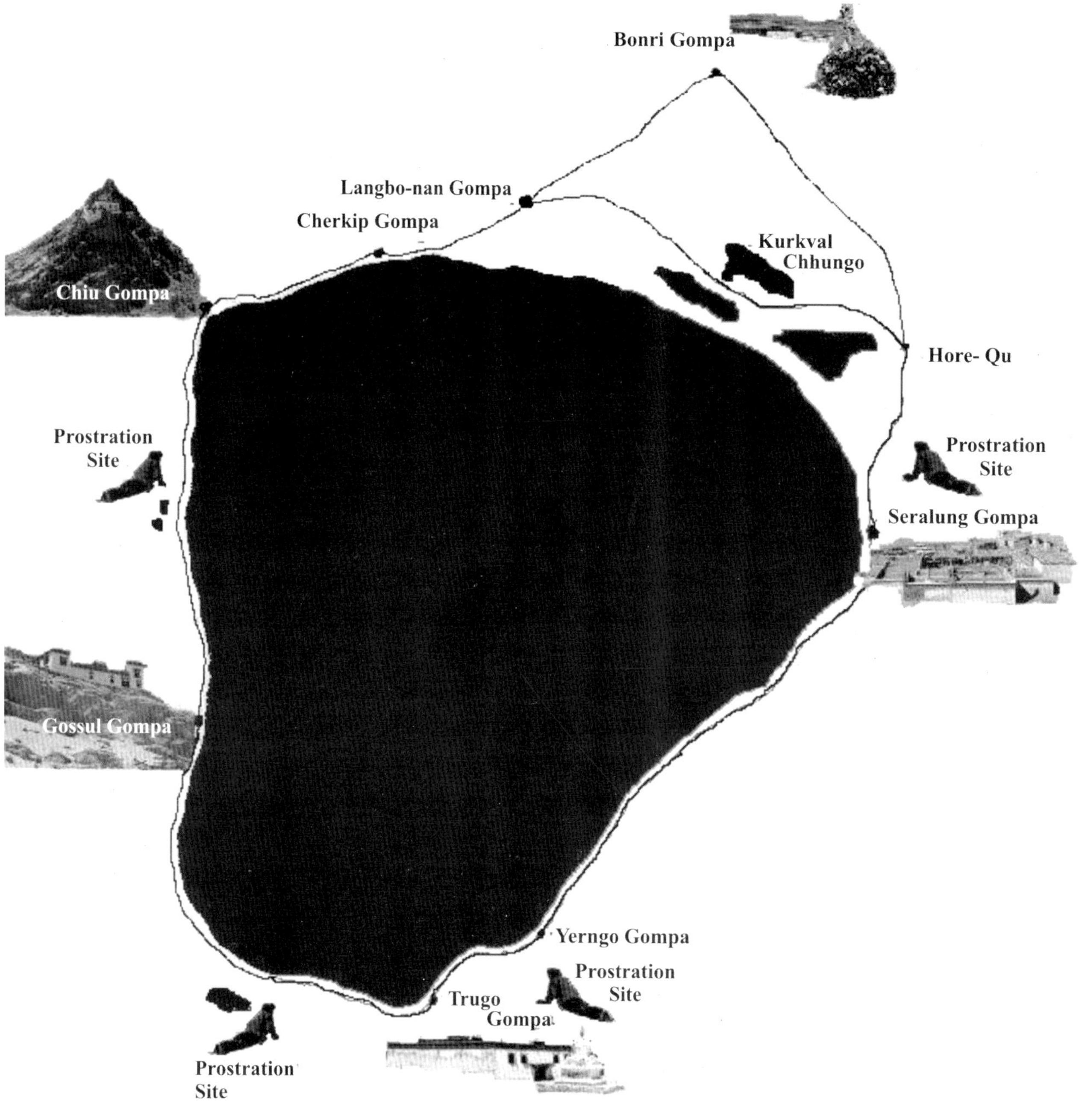

1 Pilgrimage and its Importance

Pilgrimage forms an important part of all the major religious traditions of the world. It seems to have come into vogue in India earlier than elsewhere in the world. For instance, there are indications that the people of Indus Civilization may have been practising pilgrimage as early as 2500 BCE. Later, this practice seems to have been adopted by Brahmanical Hinduism, Jainism, and Buddhism. Within these three religions pilgrimage attained to special heights and assumed a very unique and distinctive character.

Like the Indians, the Bönpos of Tibet have also been practising pilgrimage since ancient times. The arrival of Buddhism and establishment of Lamaism in Tibet provided a unique opportunity for the intermixing of Bön and Buddhist *Weltanschauung*. The institution of pilgrimage played an extremely important role in this process. Bönpo shamans and Buddhist lamas together carried pilgrimage to such pompous and glorious heights that it would be impossible to imagine pre-modern Tibet without pilgrimage. As a matter of fact, all aspects of Tibetan society became inextricably linked to pilgrimage. Thus, a typical Tibetan family would often embark on pilgrimage with all its livestock, tents, and other household goods. On the way, the family would visit various shrines, do business, and find spouses for the eligible members. Such trips typically took as much as two years. Interestingly, when Tibet was closed to foreigners in the pre-1959 period, outsiders could only enter under the pretence of pilgrimage. Thus, it is not surprising that people such as the great explorer Sven Hedin and innumerable spies of the British Raj entered Tibet disguised as pilgrims. Tibetan pilgrimage attained its uniqueness also from the fact that there were no roads or vehicles of any type in Tibet. Hence, Tibetan pilgrims had to simply trudge across huge distances. And, of course, this had to be done in a rarefied atmosphere and harsh terrain. Despite efforts by the Chinese authorities to portray pilgrimage as a sign of primitiveness and wastage, it continues to be extremely popular among the Tibetans. In India too, despite modernization and globalization and the growth of rational thinking, pilgrimage remains as popular as ever. The number of pilgrimage sites in India and Tibet is so large that the whole of Indo-Tibetan region may truly be called a grand sacred space.

To the Indians, pilgrimage is known as *tirthayatra*. It means a devotional act of journeying (*yatra*) to a sacred spot (*tirtha*). The oldest Hindu text, the *Rig Veda*, uses the term *tirtha* to describe a sacred spot associated with a body of water, such as a river ford, steps to a river, or an area associated with water. The Vedas speak of *tirtha*s as places imbued with special spiritual powers, visits to which are considered meritorious. Following the Vedic period the term *tirtha* began to be used more liberally. For instance, the great epic *Mahabharata* (400 BCE), uses it to denote any holy place, be it a lake, mountain, cave, or a confluence of two rivers. The *Mahabharata* mentions more than 300 *tirtha*s spread over the whole of Indo-Tibetan region.

The primary importance of a *tirtha* lies in the fact that it is much more than a physical and topographical site. It 'is always a special point of the earth's surface endowed with a powerful mystique' (Dowman 1988: 3) and a 'focal point of energy' imbued with sacred visions, spiritual dimensions, and healing powers. A *tirtha* serves a two-way purpose by acting as a threshold between the earth (human world) and the heaven (the world of the gods). First, a *tirtha* works as a gateway for the downward descent of various divine beings. These descending divinities are the well-known *avatara*s and *bodhisattva*s. Second, a *tirtha* acts as a door opened by an *avatara* or a *bodhisattva* through which men and women may ascend in their prayers and rites. In other words, the full meaning of the term *tirtha* is that it is a spiritual ford where heaven and earth meet and from where a spiritual person crosses the ocean of *samsara* (unending cycle of birth, death, and rebirth) and reaches the distant shore of liberation (*nirvana* or *moksa* depending upon his/her religious inclination). Thus, *tirtha*s are perceived as 'sin-destroying localities' (Chan 1994: 36).

How did the various *tirtha*s come into origin and grow into prominence? Since prehistoric times, Indians have viewed, among other things, water bodies, mountains, and river fords to be the abodes of divine beings and/or spirits. With the passage of time, different religious traditions developed various myths and legends through their association with these spots and with the great acts and appearances of various divine beings and/or spirits who had/have been dwelling there. 'Just as a field of the magnetic force is formed around a magnet, similarly there is formed a field of spiritual vibrations in those places where sages had lived and did *tapas*' (Pranavananda 1949: 5). Some of these divine beings and spirits also grew into great heroic characters. In other words, it may be said that a *tirtha* is a place where one or more divinities or heroic personalities were born, died or performed some superhuman deed, or a shrine where a particular deity had already signified it to be its pleasure to perform miracles. Saintly individuals who lead exemplary lives imbue their environments with holiness flowing from their spiritual practices. The devotees of these saintly personalities continue to derive spiritual inspiration even after their death. They do so by visiting those places which were associated with the saintly personalities. As time goes by, many folk tales about the lives of these personalities metamorphose into legends and sometimes even miracles are reported. Thus, more and more pilgrims are drawn to these spots from far and wide. The Kumbha Mela of 2001, for instance, drew as many as seventy million devotees, the largest ever gathering of humans at one place! Similarly, large gatherings of people throughout the year venerate Kapilavastu where Gautama Buddha was born, Bodhgaya where he attained Enlightenment, Sarnath where he delivered his first sermon, and Kushinagar where he died. It goes without saying that pilgrimage has permeated the lives of the Indo-Tibetan peoples to such an extent that it continues to affect the lives of most of them either directly or indirectly.

Religiously speaking, 'pilgrimage is a transaction, an investment in the future' (McKay 1998: 2). Thus, for a Hindu *tirthayatra* is one of the five constant sacred duties (*panca nitya karmas*), the other four being *dharma* (righteousness), *utsavas* (festivals), *samskaras* (sacraments), and *upasana* (devotional worship). Most of the pilgrims take a short break, of a few days to a few weeks, from their normal daily affairs and return to those affairs following the completion of their pilgrimage. Others however, spend many years, perhaps all the remaining time of their lives, wandering to the thousands of sacred sites across India. These life-time pilgrims generally fall into two distinct groups: first and quite visible, the sadhus (renunciatory ascetics) who are members of numerous different semi-monastic orders, and second, the elderly men and women who, having completed the responsibilities of raising and supporting children, have chosen to lead their final years visiting the shrines of the deities. At the shrines pilgrims find not only free or inexpensive lodgings and food but also the companionship of other wandering pilgrims.

The most striking feature of pilgrimage as a physical act is the movement of pilgrim in earthly space. Of course, if the pilgrimage spot is closer to the residence of the pilgrim, the movement shall be short-term and short-distance. But it is perceived that the merit earned from the pilgrimage would be greater if the same pilgrimage spot is farther from the residence of the pilgrim and even better if it is littered with geographical features operating as physical obstructions. The various geographical features, besides bringing merit to the pilgrim, are viewed as providing protection by warding off hostile forces. Interestingly, the merit accrued from pilgrimage gets enhanced if besides the long distance and time taken, it involves undergoing and overcoming life-threatening situations. Thus, the arduous journey and the accompanying hardships and perils undergone by a pilgrim on the way bring correspondingly greater reward. In other words, the spiritual and physical endurance presented by the journey is perceived as directly proportional to merit-making and the alleviation of sin. Thus, mishaps, extremities of weather (including sub-zero temperatures, snow storms, bitter cold, and blazing sun), bad roads, devastating landslides, avalanches, flooding, torrential rains, turbulent rivers, swept away bridges, hunger and thirst, dangerous passes over high ranges, and occasional attacks by bandits and wild animals are generally seen as enhancing the value and merits of pilgrimage. 'Both the vitality and vulnerability of the traveller give the journey the character of an initiation... the self-inflicted pain to gain entrance into a new physical and metaphysical purification' (Lemaire 1970: 99). In other words, natural and man-made hardships are perceived as instruments that help in cleansing the mind and the body of a pilgrim. Thus, for obvious reasons a genuine pilgrim is expected to choose a more prolonged and arduous route. In the classical Christian pilgrimage hardships and ordeals suffered during pilgrimage were considered so important that sometimes pilgrims carried stones on their backs. Thus, Christian pilgrims were expected to 'travel far barefoot and nowhere pass a second night and fast and watch much and pray fervently, by day and by night and willingly undergo fatigue and be so squalid that iron come not on hair or on nail' (Thorpe 1840: 411-12).

It is believed that one's death while on pilgrimage brings one the highest merit. Moreover, a pilgrim is also supposed to accept hardships uncomplainingly. Hence, in the Indo-Tibetan pilgrimage, walking is considered more meritorious than riding an animal or journeying in a vehicle to the holy spot. In other words, it is more like, say, scaling a mountain, where you would lose all the charm (read 'merit' for pilgrimage) if you were dropped on top by helicopter than climbing in the usual fashion. Thus, it is not surprising that considerable distance and extremely difficult accessibility have played an important role in making Mt Kailash a classical pilgrimage destination. Sven Hedin mentions in his travelogue of having 'met a caravan of thirty-five pilgrims from Nakchu, who, with six hundred sheep and one hundred yaks, had been to the holy mountain of Gang Rimpoche (Kailash), and were travelling so slowly that the round trip took two years' (Hedin 1925: 403). Similarly, H. Tichy, a German, met a bunch of emaciated Sri Lankans who had been travelling for over three years on their way to Mt Kailash (McKay 1998: 46).

Of course, now the pilgrimage routes in Tibet have been replaced by Chinese-built dusty highways. The Tibetan pilgrims mostly arrive atop rickety cargo trucks to Kailash. The Indian pilgrims arrive from Lipu Lekh in the comfort of a bus. The Indians who come via Nepal through the Zhangmu crossing do not have to walk even an inch till they arrive at their destination in the luxury of 4WD Toyota vehicles.

All that the Indian pilgrims now do is to perform the entire *parikrama* (circumambulation) of Manasarovar by vehicles. About a quarter of the Kailash *parikrama* is also done by vehicles. Thus, if one were to compare the modern pilgrims with those of yesteryears, it may be said that with distances shortened by modern transportation, the commitment of pilgrims has correspondingly diminished. And so has the merit, it seems! The pilgrims of the past used to arrive slowly, travelling on foot from the farthest reaches of Tibet and India. Some used to prostrate all the way in a supreme act of devotion, measuring the entire holy path with the length of their bodies. Such a practice is known as *sashtang dand pradakshina* to the Indians and the Tibetans call it *kyang khor* or *kyang chak*, i.e., the method of successive prostration on the entire circuit, each prostration beginning where the preceding one ended. It may be pointed out that the history of Kailash pilgrimage is replete with references to a large number of Indian sadhus who dressed only in kafanis traversed barefoot through the Himalayas and performed their pilgrimage. However, these days most of the pilgrims get themselves transported in vehicles like clothes in a suitcase, neither seeing nor hearing anything other than the noise of the vehicles carrying them to their destinations. In such a situation, spiritual interest gets a backseat, if not ignored altogether.

Pilgrimage also has its moral and ethical aspect. Thus, during the period of the pilgrimage, a pilgrim is expected to perform austerities (*dhutangas*), follow a code of conduct regarding food and dress, and perform various rituals including daily *upasana* and bath. Riding an animal on the way to the *tirtha* or while performing the *parikrama* is considered a violation of the spirit of pilgrimage. Unless the pilgrim is physically infirm, riding an animal, it is believed, reduces the degree of merit. Most sources seem to agree that the animal gets a share in the merit earned by the pilgrim who rides it. A pilgrim is also expected to perform acts of charity. Indians are expected to avoid the use of leather garments and shoes. During and while preparing for the pilgrimage, sadhus have to fast.

All the halting-points on the Kailash-Manasarovar route on the Indian side of the border have temples and shrines. The pilgrims are expected to rise early in the morning for the first *upasana*. Before going to sleep, they are also expected to offer the evening *upasana*. Except some of the hardcore ones, most Indian pilgrims are generally satisfied with the evening *upasana* at the Gunji and Kalapani temples which are well maintained by the Indo-Tibetan Border Police (ITBP). The evening *upasana* ceremonies at these two temples are performed through chanting, wild drumming, and singing. In this they are enthusiastically helped by the soldier-priests of the ITBP. Of course, before or after this wild singing some of the pilgrims manage to find time for a silent prayer in one of the dimly lit corners of the two temples. All pilgrims are expected to avoid liquor and refrain from eating meat as well as vegetables that smell, such as garlic and onions. But nowadays not many pilgrims observe such taboos. Brothels and liquor shops in the Tibetan towns of Taklakot, Hor Qu, and Darchen attract sufficient clientele to prosper. In fact, the disco parlours and brothels of Taklakot seem to get good business through their Indian patrons.

Timing is an important, if not paramount, aspect of pilgrimage. Though some of the *tirtha*s are visited by pilgrims throughout the year, visits on special days or occasions are supposed to carry more merit. Thus, paying a visit to a shrine on the day of a holy festival or in a particular year enhances the religious experience because on such occasions the concerned shrine is charged with greater divine significance and energy. Hence, it is believed that merit earned as a result of the Kailash pilgrimage performed during a Kumbh or horse-year (for instance, the year 2002) is twelve times more than in another year. The holy shrines at Kailash and Manasarovar offer even greater indulgence or remission from sin if visited on the 15th of the 4th month, which is a very important day in the Buddhist calendar.

Ritual bathing is an integral part of Indian pilgrimage though for the Tibetans it does not seem to hold any importance. Since prehistoric times, Indians have viewed water as containing purificatory qualities. Almost all Indian pilgrims make it a point to have a ritual bath in the freezing waters of Manasarovar and sometimes even Gauri Kund. They believe that such a bath brings both spiritual and physical healing. The medicinal, magical, and supernatural properties of the waters of these two lakes are valued so much that almost all the returning pilgrims undergo enormous hardships in carrying home some quantity of the holy water. In fact, the most precious thing that pilgrims bring with them from a pilgrimage is the holy water for consumption and anointing.

Parikrama is another important component of pilgrimage. It is a religious practice of high antiquity in India which is performed by passing clockwise around a person of reverence or holy object. It is called *pradakshina* (to go round keeping the object of reverence on the right). This practice is equally old in Tibet where it is known as *kora*. Unlike Hindus, Jainas, and Buddhists, the Tibetan Bönpos do the kora anti-clockwise. For the Tibetan pilgrims the ritual *kora* of Mt Kailash is the central activity of their pilgrimage. In strict contrast to this, for the Indian pilgrims the primary intention of their visit to a *tirtha* is to venerate the sacred place and to receive the *darshan* of the deity. The term *darshan* means seeing and/or having a spiritual communion with a deity. This deity may be resident in the form of an image, statue, or icon in a temple's inner sanctum or in an open-air shrine. The image of the deity may be either an iconic or an aniconic form symbolizing the deity. In fact, in many well-known shrines no statues of the deities are found, but only aniconic blocks of stone or such other material. The rituals followed by the Tibetans while doing the *kora* are prostrations (*chaktsal*), offerings and the recitation of *mantra*, during which they follow the instructions prescribed by the pilgrimage treatises.

Indian pilgrims do the *parikrama* of Manasarovar in vehicles and that of Kailash partly in vehicles and partly by riding ponies and yaks. Only a few of them manage to do the *parikrama* of Kailash on foot. Failure to do the *parikrama* due to inclement weather or bad health is not really viewed by the Indian pilgrims as resulting in incomplete pilgrimage. Tibetan pilgrims believe that it is only by doing the *parikrama* of Mt Kailash that they could hope to attain spiritual purification leading to the ultimate liberation. Nonetheless, the potential for enlightenment, which, according to Buddhist belief, all sentient beings possess, is activated by the mere sight of Kailash.

The *Vinaya Pitaka*, a Buddhist text of fifth century BCE, considers *parikrama*, prostrations, and making offerings during pilgrimage as spiritually significant. And if this is done on certain auspicious days, the merit thus gained is believed to be a hundred or even a thousand times greater. However, it may be interesting to ask if guides and porters earn individual merit and/or get a share in the merit earned by the pilgrim whose goods they transport on the *parikrama*. Porters, pony herders, and guides certainly do not go around the holy object with spirituality in mind. Same could be said of the adventure tourists. Some of the sources seem to give the impression that if reverence is lacking then nothing is gained by mere circling and thus a porter or a guide who does the *parikrama* for money does not get any merit from it. However, this does not seem to apply to the substitutes hired to perform the arduous journey for the indolent or the ill. In such a case the religious merit earned is shared between the sponsor and he who actually walks along the path, provided, of course, the latter has undertaken the job as a pilgrim. But, to earn full merit, we are told, there can be no substitution. It may also be interesting to see in the case of Hindu pilgrims as to whether merit earned by them gets reduced in the absence of a daily ritual bath. Almost all the pilgrims miss their daily bath while doing the *parikrama* of Kailash as it is extremely cold.

Parikrama by prostration (*sashtang dand pradakshina*) is a powerful way of showing devotion. No Indian is known to have done the *parikrama* of Kailash by prostration. But the Tibetans do it in fairly good numbers. Some even do their *kora* sideways, advancing one side step at a time while facing the holy object. Most Tibetans prefer to do the *kora* of Kailash in a single day, a feat lasting fifteen to seventeen hours due to uneven terrain, altitude sickness, and harsh conditions. (Reinhold Messner is said to have completed the entire *kora* in twelve hours!) It is known as *nyimo-kora* (afternoon *parikrama*) or even *khyi-kora* (dog *parikrama*) for the great hurry with which it is performed. Talking about the unseemly hurry, it was pointed out by a visitor to Tibet towards the beginning of the twentieth century that 'one and all condemn the record-breaker, who hurries round in as short a time as possible, and they apply to him the opprobrious epithet of *khi-kora*, the man who runs round like a dog' (Sherring 1906: 280). However, most Tibetans now believe that *khyi-kora* is an efficient means of earning merit as it is easier than walking two or three days saddled with luggage.

It is believed that the merit earned through *parikrama* by prostration is eight times more than the same done on foot. This form of *parikrama* of Kailash takes up to four weeks in the open. Pilgrims are not allowed to skip difficult parts, like frozen ground or streams. In Tibet, 'the country people believe that if they make the... *kora* once, they will be absolved of ordinary sins. To be cleared of murder, two *kora*s are required, but if the round is completed thrice, even the murder of a father or mother will be atoned for' (Rawat 1973: 48). We are further told that ten *kora*s can purify the defilement of one *kalpa* (aeon), after one hundred *kora*s a pilgrim will attain Enlightenment in one life time, and instant *nirvana* is guaranteed after 108 *parikrama*s. Most Tibetans consider at least three circuits as bare minimum, though thirteen is considered quite desirable as this makes pilgrims eligible for the prestigious inner *kora* (*nangkor*). Those who have not done at least thirteen *parikramas* of Kailash, it is considered a sacrilege for them to either do the inner *kora* or take a short-cut via the Khando Sangam-la.

A Tibetan Pilgrim doing the *saṣṭāṅga daṇḍa pradakṣiṇā* of Mt Kailash

Interestingly, most religious traditions recognize proxy in pilgrimage. Where someone is unable to undertake the journey for reasons of illness, frailty or otherwise he is permitted to arrange with someone else to perform the journey on his behalf. Thus, proxy pilgrims are sent. In some cases Tibetans would carry a ribbon-decorated sheep as a proxy for a family member left behind. Some Indian pilgrims also carry cash and gifts from their friends and relatives to be cast off into Manasarovar after the ritual bath at Trugo Gompa. The Indo-Tibetan religious traditions also recognize a share in as well as transfer of merit earned through the performance of pilgrimage. Thus, Indian pilgrims perform *yajnas*, offer ritual giving (*dana*), and take dips in the cold waters of the Manasarovar in the name of relatives and friends, both deceased and living.

Though people of all religions go on pilgrimage to wipe out sins, many of them believe that the deity or deities who reside in the *tirthas* are able to fulfil their wishes. Thus, arduous journeys are undertaken to seek encouragement, solace, guidance, or inspiration. Many Indian pilgrims travel to their deities to ask for supernatural aid to end a spate of bad luck, or for curing an illness. Others go to seek their deity's aid in the fulfilment of long held dreams. Some unmarried women go seeking a husband and the jobless a job. Some others go seeking a male heir. After securing a victory in an election or getting charge of a coveted ministry, many politicians in India are known to go on pilgrimage for thanksgiving. Some pilgrims go to discharge a religious obligation, because of a prior vow to make a pilgrimage if the deity granted a wish. Some go on pilgrimage to say their thanks for the 'extra assistance' that their deity rendered them in fulfilling wishes and dreams. Extreme poverty appears to have been an important cause for inspiring Tibetan pilgrimage. A majority of the Tibetans have always been at the mercy of nature and it is not unusual for people to die during the winter months due to non-availability of food. In times of hardship the help or forgiveness of one's deity is often invoked and a promise is made that a pilgrimage would be undertaken to the invoked god/goddess/saint's shrine for the favour. Thus, in the belief that various natural as well as unnatural calamities (including Communist takeover) could be a physical manifestation of divine wrath, Tibetans go on pilgrimage to beg forgiveness, or indeed to give thanks for having survived Chinese atrocities.

Pilgrimage also carries penitential significance. A large number of people go on pilgrimage to seek forgiveness for a moral or ethical sin or legal crime. The purpose of penitential pilgrimage is for the salvation of transgressors, even for salvation of the soul/being of their victims if the crime has been murder. This means that the resident deity is seen as having the power to grant forgiveness to pilgrims for their past, present, and future sins, thus saving them from torments in hell through a better rebirth or even a place in heaven. Many sadhus undertake the vows of abandonment by formally renouncing all ties and embracing pilgrimage as a full-time occupation. For such and other spiritual pilgrims, the rewards refer to the journey from ignorance to Enlightenment and culminating in liberation from the cycle of birth, death, and rebirth.

In some cases, very different urges and incentives for pilgrimage seem to be at work. Thus, some pilgrims nowadays consider pilgrimage as an excuse for a spring excursion. It offers them the chance to get away from reality, break the routine and to experience some level of freedom from domestic constraints, meet new people, and interact with new cultures. Apart from escapism, the experience of moving into an unfamiliar environment certainly inspires feelings of great anticipation and emotion among some pilgrims. Pilgrimage offers a chance for reflection and revaluation of life in a way not normally possible in domestic routine. Pilgrimage may also offer a quest for adventure and psychological healing, not to speak of spiritual purification. There are some places one goes not only to rest, or to slow the march of time, or to contemplate the power of nature, but to make a pilgrimage into one's self. 'When you travel, you experience, in a very spiritual way, the act of rebirth. You confront completely new situations, the day passes more slowly, and on most journeys you don't even understand the language the people speak... and you accept any small favour from the gods with great delight, as if it were an episode you would remember for the rest of your life' (Coehlo 1997). Thus, whereas for some pilgrimage is an inspiring and uplifting experience, for others it is introspective and humbling. The ever present dangers and struggles of modern life also seem to persuade quite a few persons to go on pilgrimage. However, pilgrimage is not always undertaken for the best of motives. Thus, even when begun in good faith at times, pilgrimage is known to have degraded into occasions of vice. In the pre-1959 period, bandits in western Tibet used to commit robberies and murder innocent people believing that in the end a few rounds of the holy Kailash would absolve them of all their ugly karma. In India, notorious gangsters and criminals are known to go on pilgrimage to evade arrest. Moreover, in the present times, the terms 'pilgrim' and 'pilgrimage' have come to acquire a somewhat devalued meaning, and are often applied in a secular context. For example, fans of a political leader may choose to visit his grave and call it a pilgrimage!

Common masses have always believed that to receive or assist a pilgrim is to share in the merit and virtue of his journey. Thus, Hindu-Buddhist practices of charity (*maitri, karuna*) and alms-giving (*bhiksha*) invented a method of participating in the merits of a pilgrimage for those unable to take part in it. Thus, both secular and religious organizations providing support to pilgrims in various forms have existed in the Indo-Tibetan region since ancient times. For instance, inns came into existence in India as early as the third century BCE. Further, monastic institutions have always provided not only food and shelter to roving monks and nuns, but have also acted as open houses to all types and classes of pilgrims, including the poor and foreigners. Interestingly, pilgrims are also known to have indulged in merit enhancing activities while on pilgrimage, for example, acting as postmen carrying letters from place to place as they went.

Pilgrimage holds significant economic importance as it gives boost to various commercial activities. The high mobility of people in the context of pilgrimage, the scale at which it takes place as well as the vast distances covered by the pilgrims, all contribute to the likelihood of trade. In fact, a majority of the nomadic people in Tibet till recent times have been (and some still are) pilgrims and it is not easy to isolate pilgrimage from their socio-economic life in general. In the pre-1959 period, pilgrims in Tibet used to be away for a long period of time and many of them used to barter their way to the destination. The pilgrimage of farmers and herders was often combined with petty trade. They used to carry their agricultural surplus in the form of bundles of tea, parcels of gold dust, and silver ingots. In fact, these pilgrims also employed their sheep, yaks, and other cattle as a sort of walking merchandise. Thus, not only material and spiritual goals of many pilgrims coincided and still do, but *tirtha*s and *mandis* (trading fairs) also often overlap. The economic existence of numerous lay travellers also revolves around business activities at pilgrimage sites.

Kailash pilgrimage has become an important event of commercial importance. At towns such as Darchen, hotels, shops, restaurants, and other commercial establishments thrive primarily due to pilgrimage. Kailash pilgrimage helps greatly in western Tibet in the circulation of goods, particularly small items of value such as semi-precious stones (bought as souvenirs at Darchen and around Manasarovar). Many transporters, pony herders, horsemen, porters, and guides earn their livelihood by working for the pilgrims, thus their avocation is a matter of interest to the local authority at Dharchula in India and at Darchen in Tibet. There are others whose commercial enterprise means that they play a vital role in what could fairly be described as the pilgrimage 'industry', such as market vendors, taverners, souvenir sellers, hostel and hospital workers, transporters, and pony owners. Kumaon Mandal Vikas Nigam (KMVN) has set up a large number of guesthouses on the Indian side of the Kailash pilgrimage route to cater to the needs of the pilgrims.

Kailash pilgrimage has also acquired great importance for both the secular and religious authorities in India who in turn seek to control and influence the pilgrims. Some of the members of Indian Parliament raise questions from time to time enquiring about various aspects of the Kailash pilgrimage. In fact, the Indian government makes fixed donations to the KMVN as well as to the Indo-Tibetan Border Police (ITBP) to defray part of the costs of the Kailash pilgrims. Provincial governments of states such as Delhi and Gujarat offer liberal cash support and travel gear to their domiciled pilgrims. Various religious organizations offer free food materials for the journey apart from the tumultuous receptions, meals, and religious literature. The Indian Ministry of External Affairs, ITBP, and some private organizations in India give the pilgrims medallions, badges, or certificates stamped with the symbol of the shrine so that they and others would know that they had been on the pilgrimage. Some pilgrims actually add the title 'Kailashi' to their names after the successful conclusion of pilgrimage to Mt Kailash.

The Government of India maintains a tight control over this pilgrimage. As all the trekking on the Indian side takes place in notified territory, pilgrims have to apply for a permit from the Government of India to pass through this region. The Ministry of External Affairs makes selection of the pilgrims and appoints its Liaison Officer to lead each batch on pilgrimage. This ministry also negotiates with the Chinese government from time to time regarding management of the pilgrimage in Tibet. Through the process of systemization, the Government of India in coordination with KMVN and ITBP has also been establishing institutions to house, feed, and instruct pilgrims.

The origin and growth of Buddhism in India in the fifth century BCE injected a new meaning into the institution of pilgrimage. After his Enlightenment at Bodhgaya, the Buddha spent the

A momento given by the ITBP to the returning pilgrims

remaining forty-five years of his earthly life in travel and advised his disciples to be wanderers. For instance, in the *Mahaparinibbana Suttanta* the Buddha tells his chief disciple, Ananda, that there are four places which 'a devout person should visit and look upon with reverence'. These four places are Lumbini (his birthplace), Bodhgaya (place of Enlightenment), Sarnath (place of first sermon), and Kushinagar (place of Mahaparinirvana). These four places became known as the *Caturmahapratiharya*s (the Four Great Wonders) and pilgrims began to visit them. Soon, four more talons associated with the Buddha's life also became pilgrimage sites and together the eight places became known as *Astamahapratiharya*s (the Eight Great Wonders). These four sites are Rajgir (place where he tamed a maddened elephant), Shravasti (the site of a momentous event known as the Miracle of the Pairs), Vaishali (place where monkeys offered him a gift of honey), and Sankasya (the place where he descended from Heaven after preaching to his mother). Emperor Ashoka also made significant contribution to the tradition of Buddhist pilgrimage. His religious fervour coupled with the force of his imperial patronage initiated and sanctioned both a sacred geography and a pilgrimage practice in India. This tradition was further perpetuated by monks such as Padmasambhava, who established Buddhism in Tibet.

KMY/13/2004 8th September, 2004

CERTIFICATE

This is to certify that Shri KARAM TEJ SINGH SARAO participated in the Kailash Mansarovar Yatra, 2004, organised by the Ministry of External Affairs. He was a member of the thirteenth batch, which undertook the Yatra from 09.08.2004 to 07.09.2004.

2. The Indian Mountaineering Foundation (IMF) has recognised the Kailash Mansarovar Yatra as a trekking expedition, for which Government servants are eligible for grant of special casual leave as per notification issued by Ministry of Personnel & Training vide O.M. No. [illegible] dated April 11, 1985.

(PRASAY K. VERMA)
DEPUTY SECRETARY (CHINA)

Completion certificate given by the Ministry of External Affairs to pilgrims who successfully complete their pilgrimage

It is important to note that pilgrimage, which is a universal feature of Tibetan society, has played an important role in the very survival of Tibetans as a nationality with a unique culture. 'By going on pilgrimages, Tibetans seem to assert their identity; wandering along the pilgrimage routes, they map out their territory anew and re-appropriate their space in the face of the Chinese occupation' (Buffetrille 1998: 30). Over half a century of repression by the Chinese Communist regime does not seem to have reduced the religious fervour of the Tibetan people. However, Chinese rule has set in some very serious and irreversible changes into the very institution of pilgrimage. Contradictions have arisen between modern economic needs and traditional practices; between spiritual merit and material gain; and between the needs to reaffirm identity and the need to make money. Pilgrimage and tourist seasons overlap. As a result, the number of Tibetans undertaking pilgrimage has significantly declined as the local people prefer to take advantage of the economic opportunities offered by the tourist trade rather than undertaking pilgrimages. As a consequence of the Chinese occupation, individual mobility has also been greatly

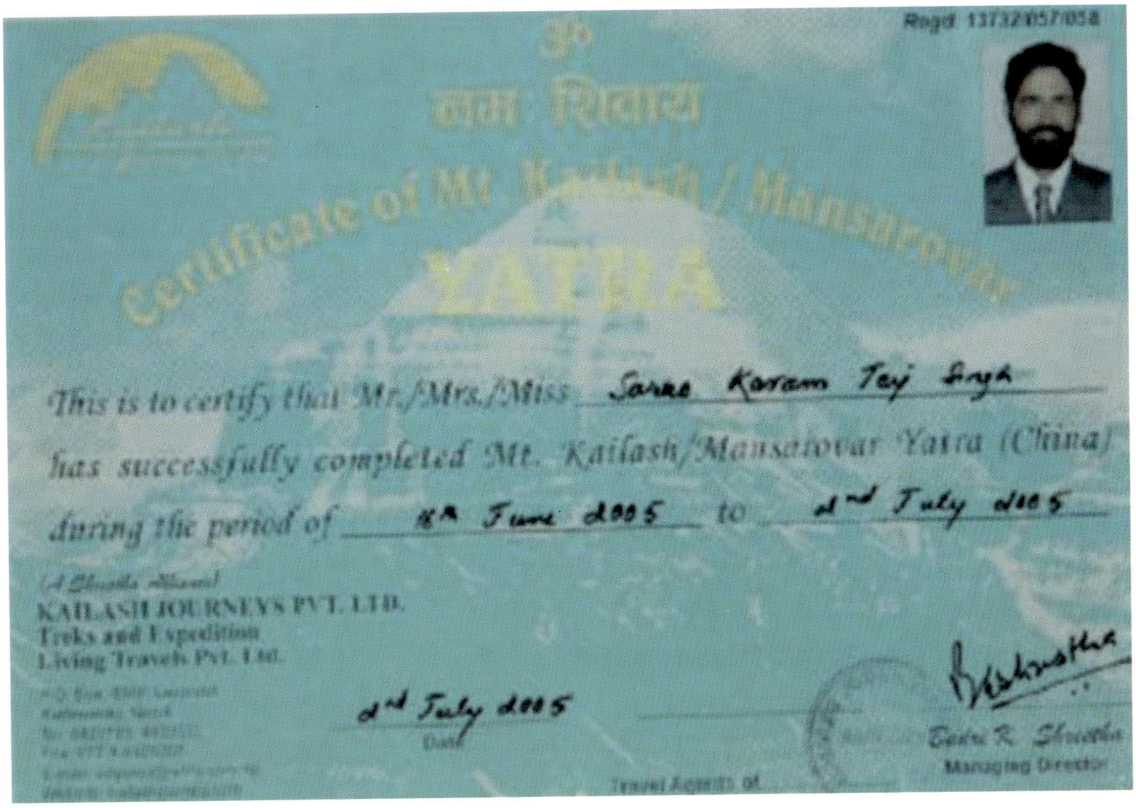

Private Tour Agencies also give completion certificates to pilgrims who do their pilgrimage via Nepal

reduced and many local practices have been brought to a halt. Pilgrimage is condemned by the Communist rulers not only as 'feudal remains' but also as 'waste of time' which is 'harmful' to production.

As compared to Tibet, however, pilgrimage has continued uninterrupted in India. Ever since the Indians marched into the twilight zone of civilization, the region of the Himalayas and beyond has been considered as the most suitable for practising austerities. Since then Indian sadhus have been drawn to this region. In the Indian ascetical tradition it is believed that in order to attain profound spiritual vision one must meditate and practise severe austerities by leading a life away from the mundane world of the ordinary. Leading a life in complete isolation and under extreme conditions requires mental and physical discipline of the highest order. Thus, it is not surprising that the trans-Himalayan region of Mt Kailash and Manasarovar is viewed as the ultimate place of extraordinary and superhuman endeavour. For instance, when Arjuna arrives at the boundaries of the Himalayas this fact is made clear to him in full measure. He is reminded that this is a place where 'a mortal man cannot disport himself' (*Mahabharata*.III.152.5-10) and where 'one who has failed in austerities cannot reach' (*Mahabharata*.III.142.25-30). In fact, this region is viewed as being 'beyond the course of humans' (*Mahabharata*.III.156.21-23). Within this kind of thinking Kailash-Manasarovar became the ultimate goal for ascetics. The extreme climatic conditions, rarefied atmosphere, and difficult terrain have added to the sublime beauty of Kailash and Manasarovar to such an extent that even many self-professed nonbelievers are known to have been deeply touched by their sight and some have even been moved to tears of joy by the sheer impression of these spots. Many semi-pilgrims are drawn to the Kailash-Manasarovar region not only because such a venture involves serious risk, but also because this journey poses considerable challenge to one's endurance and patience.

Pali and Sanskrit literature mentions western Tibet as Uttarakuru. A detailed description of this semi-mythical and semi-historical region is given in the *Atanatiya Sutta* (*Dīgha Nikāya*.iii.199ff. See also Hopkins 1968: 186). According to this description, the people of this region did not own any property nor did men have wives of their own. People did not have to work for their living as food grew of its own. The inhabitants went about riding on cows, on men and women, on maids and youths. Their king rode on an elephant, on a horse, on celestial cars and in state palanquins. Their cities were built in the air, and Alakananda was their chief city. The king of Uttarakuru is Kuvera (also called Vessavana). Mention is also made of a lake named Dharani and a hall named Bhagalavati where the Yakkhas, as the inhabitants of Uttarakuru are called, hold their assemblies. The region, eight thousand leagues in extent, is always spoken of as being to the north of Jambudipa (South Asia) and as one of the four continents, the other three being Aparagoyana, Pubbavideha, and Jambudipa (*Aṅguttara Nikāya*.I.227; V.59; *Dīgha Nikāya Aṭṭhakathā*.II.623; *Buddhavaṃsa Aṭṭhakathā*.113; *Sutta-Nipāta Aṭṭhakathā*.II.443). These four make up a Cakkavala, with Mt Meru in their midst, a flat-world system. A cakkavatti's rule extends over all these four continents (*Dīgha Nikāya*.II.173; *Dīgha Nikāya Aṭṭhakathā*.II.623) and his chief queen comes either from the race of King Madda (of Punjab) or from Uttarakuru; in the latter case she appears before him of her own accord, urged on by her good fortune (*Dīgha Nikāya Aṭṭhakathā*.II.626; *Khuddaka-Pāṭha Aṭṭhakathā*.173). The trees in Uttarakuru bear perpetual fruit and foliage, and it also possesses a Kapparukkha which lasts for a whole *kappa* (*Aṅguttara Nikāya*.I.264; *Majjhima Nikāya Aṭṭhakathā*.II.948). There are no houses in Uttarakuru, the inhabitants sleep on the earth and are called, therefore, *bhumisaya* (earth-sleepers) (*Theragāthā Aṭṭhakathā*.II.187f). The men of Uttarakuru surpass even the gods of Tavatimsa in four things: (a) they have no greed (*amama*) (*Vibhaṅga Aṭṭhakathā*.461), (b) no private property (*apariggaha*), (c) they have a definite term of life (*niyatayuka*), one thousand years, after which they are born in heaven (*Aṅguttara Nikāya Aṭṭhakathā*.II.8), and (d) they possess great elegance (*visesabhuno*). They are, however, inferior to the men of Jambudipa in courage, mindfulness and religious life (*Aṅguttara Nikāya*.IV.396; *Kathāvatthu*.99). Several instances are given of the Buddha having gone to Uttarakuru for alms. Having obtained his food there, he would go to the Anotatta lake, bathe in its waters and, after the meal, spend the afternoon on its banks (*Vinaya Piṭakaṃ*.I.27-8; *Dhammapadaṭṭhakathā*.III.222). The power of going to Uttarakuru for alms is not restricted to the Buddha; Pacceka Buddhas and various ascetics are mentioned as having visited Uttarakuru on their begging rounds (*Jātaka*.V.316; VI.100; *Majjhima Nikāya Aṭṭhakathā*.I.340; *Sutta-Nipāta Aṭṭhakathā*.II.420). It is considered a mark of great *iddhi*-power to be able to do this (*Saṃyutta Nikāya Aṭṭhakathā*.I.93; *Milindapañha*.84). Jotika's wife was a woman of Uttarakuru; she was brought to Jotika by the gods. She brought with her a single pint pot of rice and three crystals. The rice-pot was never exhausted; whenever a meal was desired, the rice was put in a boiler and the boiler set over the crystals; the heat of the crystals went out as soon as the rice was cooked. The same thing happened with curries (*Dhammapadaṭṭhakathā*.IV.209ff). Food never ran short in Uttarakuru; once when there was a famine in Veranja and the Buddha and his monks were finding it difficult to get alms, we find Moggallana suggesting that they should go to Uttarakuru for alms (*Vinaya Piṭakaṃ*.III.7). The clothes worn by the inhabitants resembled divine robes (*Petavatthu Aṭṭhakathā*.76). It was natural for the men of Uttarakuru not to transgress virtue as they were endowed with *pakati-sila* (natural or proper virtue) (*Visuddhimagga*.I.15).

Geographical, religious, economic, and political factors on both sides of the Indo-Tibetan border have played an important role in the Kailash-Manasarovar pilgrimage. These factors have not only affected this pilgrimage but have also been in turn affected by it. From the Indian perspective western Tibet developed from a semi-mythical region known as Uttarakuru to the Ladakh kingdom when Zorawar Singh conquered it. From the Tibetan point of view, the Kailash-Manasarovar region developed from tribal territory to an independent kingdom. Eventually, this kingdom became part of both the greater Indian and greater Tibetan identity and sacred geography. However strange it may sound, this region did not become part of the greater Indian polity. The reason for this was that in the Indian perspective Kailash-Manasarovar were an 'ideal' pilgrimage site – a site which was so highly sanctified that it stayed out of the reach of ordinary Indian mortals. Though pilgrimages to Kailash-Manasarovar have been made since the earliest times, yet, historically, the region does not appear to have had the structures typically associated with Hindu pilgrimage sites. Such sites are usually institutionalized. They have some sort of *dharamshalas/ashramas* to house pilgrims; there are temples or at least sacred images, and there are bathing *ghats*. Resident *purohitas* (priests) advise pilgrims of the appropriate prayers to be made at the site, the most auspicious days to visit, and the type of offerings to be made there, as well as the benefits accruing from these actions. But there is no record of any such structures existing in the Kailash-Manasarovar region, at least until the 1930s. The lack of such structures may partly reflect the fact that the region has been outside the political boundaries of what is now India, although theoretically it is within Indian religious geography. It is also true that there are other Hindu pilgrimage sites without such structures. Amarnath Cave in the Himalayas also has no *ashrams* or other symbols of a pilgrimage site.

The lack of structures in the Kailash region raises a question: how many Hindu pilgrims actually visited this region in the pre-1959 period? Kailash was not seen as a destination for ordinary pilgrims. Besides the legendary hero-kings, it appears to have principally attracted sadhus (McKay, 1998: 175). These sadhus, though not necessarily an unsystematized phenomenon, were not primarily concerned with the construction of religious structures. They also stayed aloof from local political and economic matters. Added to this, the difficulties of travel, altitude, scarce resources, bandits etc. discouraged ordinary Indians from venturing into western Tibet. These factors together played their role in the historical process that resulted in the waning of Indian influence in western Tibet and the consequent development of the Tibetan national identity. Political expediency of the British Raj further helped in this process. It is in these circumstances that western Tibet (also known as Ngari or Ali), the land of Mt Kailash and Lake Manasarovar has now become firmly fixed not only within Tibetan identity but also within Tibetan borders. In the early Indian perspective it was located beyond the periphery of the ordered world, in the 'wilderness' – which might be drawn into the 'known' by the presence and power of Hindu sanyasis travelling and practising there. Interestingly, there has been an associated growth of rituals and of oral or literary traditions concerning Kailash and Manasarovar which serve to locate the pilgrimage within the Indic tradition. Thus, Vyas Ashram, Om Parvat, Dharchula, Kalinadi, and Nabhidhang have all associations with Shiva or his devotees. But this transformation process never progressed to the point where the region developed the structures associated with a Hindu pilgrimage site, although under British patronage that process had begun by the 1930s and 1940s, only to be prevented by the Chinese takeover. Kailash thus remained outside the political boundaries of India. Amongst the Indian pilgrims, one no longer sees many barefoot travellers of the past, who struggled alone through an unfamiliar, high, and hostile land. In the past the ranks of Indians who came here were selected by the strength of their devotion and limited by the difficulty of the journey. These days the process is conducted through the Ministry of External Affairs (MEA), which from a flood of applications chooses about 400 pilgrims by lottery. Most of these pilgrims are middle-aged upper caste businessmen from urban centres.

2 History of Pilgrimage to Kailash-Manasarovar

The holy mountain Kailash and the lakes Manasarovar and Rakshas Tal are located in the western Tibetan plateau between the Gurla Mandhata mountain in the southeast and Kunlun mountain in the northwest. Being in the trans-Himalayan region, the mandala created by their positions is important not only for believers, but nonbelievers also find this place incredibly enchanting. Though there are no specific references to Mt Kailash in the Vedic texts, it seems that Indians were aware of its existence. For instance, it has been mentioned in the *Rig Veda* (2.15.6.) that Lord Indra 'through his power made the Indus flow in a northern direction.' On the basis of this hymn, Frits Staal has pointed out that as the Indus flows in a northerly direction just a few kilometres from Mt Kailash. The Vedic people could hardly have failed to notice it (Staal 1990: 290). It has also been pointed out that there is evidence in the Vedic texts for the existence of ascetics who carried out spiritual practices in the Himalayas (Frawley 1995: 92). Pilgrimage may well have been one of the many features originally introduced into the Brahmanical Hindu religious system by these ascetics (McKay 1998: 168). There are also indications that many mountains in the Himalayas and beyond began to be associated with spirituality and came to be regarded as the home of Vedic deities.

Pilgrimage certainly seems to have become fairly well entrenched in the Indian society by the time the Vedic Indians established themselves in the middle Gangetic plains and sacrificial rites began to give way to alternative practices such as pilgrimage. The *Aitareya Brahmana* has perhaps the earliest textual reference to the existence of pilgrimage. Here, while praising the 'flower-like heels of the wanderer', this text points out that 'all his sins disappear, slain by the toil of his journeying' (*Aitareya Brahmana*.7-15 quoted in Bhardwaj 1973: 3). By about 1000 BCE, if not earlier, Indians must have begun to visit Kailash and Manasarovar as pilgrims. The *Ramayana* and the *Mahabharata,* which went on to 'fix the normative values of Aryan culture' (Varma 1988-89: 13) further popularized the Kailash pilgrimage in Indian society.

The five Pandava brothers and their wife, principal characters of the *Mahabharata*, are known to have embarked upon a pilgrimage to Kailash towards the end of their earthly lives. However,

Lord Shiva at Kailash as depicted in a tableau on the occasion of Shivaratri

only Yudhishthir accompanied by his faithful dog is said to have made it in the end, the rest having perished on the way. Even he lost his toe because his truthfulness had been thrown into doubt due to a paradoxical statement he had made during the Battle of Mahabharata. Similarly, Rama of the *Ramayana* is said to have paid a visit to Kailash. In the *Mahabharata* it is stated that Vyasa, the legendary systemizer of the Vedas, had also visited Kailash (Sabha Chapter: 43,17). The Buddha also encouraged his monks and nuns to constantly travel and many *Jataka* stories speak of the value of the pilgrimage to holy Meru (Mt Kailash). The inscriptions of Emperor Ashoka mention him as having given up war in favour of peace and pilgrimage in the third century BCE. During his many pilgrimages to the holy places of Buddhism, Asoka paid visits to Lumbini and Bodhgaya. Legend has it that Krishna paid a visit to Kailash. Ravana, the king of Lanka, is said to have meditated for a *kalpa* in this region at the shores of Rakas Tal, adjoining the Manasarovar, and succeeded in obtaining a boon of prowess equalling Shiva's own. According to folklore, once Ravana lifted Mt Kailash and shook it so hard that scared Parvati (who had been upset with Shiva after a quarrel) scrambled back to Shiva's arms. This scene is beautifully described in a sculpture at the Kailash Temple at Ellora.

The Kailash Temple at Ellora hewn out of a monolith

Though some scholars believe that the practice of pilgrimage began in Tibet at the earliest in the seventh century CE with the arrival of Buddhism from India (Buffetrille 1998: 19), it is almost certain that it pre-dates the arrival of Buddhism by a considerable period of time. It must be noted that in those early centuries Tibet did not exist in as much isolation as is generally believed and Indian and Tibetan cultures have been enriching each other since pre-historic times. There may have been, as R.A. Stein suggested, links between Brahmanical Hinduism and the early 'unsystematized' Bön. Such links may well have been stimulated by the presence of gold and other precious metals in the Kailash-Manasarovar region. To the followers of Bön faith, Kailash, the soul-mountain of Zhang-Zhung was an ice-capped pyramid called Gangri Tise as well as Yungdruk Gu Tseg, the 'Nine-Storeyed Swastika Mountain.' To the Bönpo, as to the Hindus, the swastika was an ancient symbol of power. On the southern face of the sacred mountain a vertical gully intersecting with horizontal striations in the rock emblazoned the sign for the faithful to see. After the arrival of Buddhism, Kailash was 'Buddhacized' in the Tibetan religious system. This process of 'Buddhacization' involved the construction of new understandings of the place through the ritual appropriation of existing sacred space, often by means of transferring concepts of sacred geography from Indian sources (Huber 1990). In this process pre-existing indigenous deities were subjugated or converted into Buddhist deities and Buddhist concepts were superimposed onto the cult of the territorial god (*yul lha*). This involved the 'mandalization' of the landscape within the Buddhist understanding (often with the *yul lha* being incorporated into the mandala as a protective deity) and an 'opening' of the sacred centre, involving the 'discovery' of the *parikrama* path by a charismatic Buddhist figure. At Kailash the territorial god though may have been subjugated but was not completely converted. Thus, the original *yul lha* deity was not completely superseded by the Buddhist deity (Milarepa) and the Indian model of *parikrama* (*pradakshina*, 'moving to the right') – an essential ritual act of Buddhist pilgrimage – continued along with the Bön *kora* of moving anti-clockwise.

Kailash Temple at Ellora: Ravana attempting to lift Kailash

The cosmologies and myths of origin of each of the four religions (Hinduism, Buddhism, Jainism, and Bön) speak of Kailash as the mythical Mt Meru, the centre and birth place of the entire universe. Pilgrimage to this mountain, undoubtedly, appears as a recurrent theme at all times in the art and literature of both India and Tibet. The Kailash pilgrimage has been systematized within each of these religious traditions. This process began when the site attracted mendicants of each faith, whose religious practices further increased the sanctity of the region in their followers' perspective. As increasing numbers of pilgrims were drawn towards it, aspects of landscape, history, myth, and text were used to identify the region as sacred within that faith.

The establishment of Anglo-Tibetan ties at the turn of the twentieth century transformed the modern pilgrimage to Kailash-Manasarovar. The British felt that pilgrims would work as harbingers of trade and commerce. Thus, they 'constructed an image of Kailash which presented it as a desirable pilgrimage centre for all types of Hindus; a construction designed to stimulate the pilgrimage in order to bring revenue to frontier districts. In the preceding centuries, however, it was apparently a site visited only by a small group of renunciates of a particular sect.' (McKay 1998: 13) 'British patronage led to dramatic increase in the numbers of Indian pilgrims to the Kailas region after the 1920s. But it appears that whereas the early pilgrims were renunciates, Kailas-Manasarovar increasingly came within the range of tours of wealthy and educated caste Hindu pilgrims, who returned to their worldly lives after their pilgrimage. What was once a land of heroes and ascetics was now open to anyone with the necessary fitness, desire, and money' (McKay 1998: 180).

Lieutenant Henry Strachey, who travelled to western Tibet in 1846, records having met two Hindu sadhus. The first, described as an 'intelligent, smart, and decent *sanyasi*,' had been roughly apprehended by the Tibetan authorities on arrival and only permitted to perform the *upasana* and ritual bathing at Manasarovar under escort. He had been refused permission to do the *parikrama* of either the lake, or of Mount Kailash. The second sadhu, whom Strachey describes as a '*yogi*' of poor appearance and a half-fool, had no such problems. Strachey attributed this to the Tibetans' not unreasonable suspicion that an intelligent sadhu could be a British agent (H. Strachey, 1848: 84). It was not so easy even for sadhus to perform pilgrimage as not only dacoits but also the Tibetan authorities created hurdles in their way. Strachey's report suggests that what we might call the 'hard core' of pilgrims to Kailash were still sadhus, and it is consistent with the textual evidence suggesting that this was, historically a renunciate pilgrimage (McKay 1998: 177). It could be that only people with resources or those 'who did not have anything to lose' took the risk to go. A family man with poor resources could not afford either the expenses or the risks and hardships. Thus, in the pre-1959 period, commoners generally avoided going on pilgrimage to Kailash. Wealthy people, however, were known sometimes to have hired others to perform the pilgrimage for them. Pilgrimage to Tibet besides being dangerous and expensive was also time-consuming. In the pre-1959 days, it used to take as much as three months. Now it can be performed in less than a month via the Lipu Lekh and in about two weeks via the Kodari-Zhangmu Pass of Nepal.

Paucity of evidence makes it almost impossible to assess the numbers of pilgrims and traders visiting Kailash and Manasarovar up to the twentieth century. It is hard, for instance, to know whether the treaty negotiated by the British at Lhasa in 1904, which gave Indian pilgrims free entry into Tibet, had any real effect upon numbers entering. In 1907, Sherring was told that about 150 sanyasins visited annually but that every twelve years during the Kumbh year up to 400 attended (Sherring, 1906: 144). Bharati gives the figure of 600 pilgrims visiting Kailash and Manasarovar in 1951 (Bharati 1963: 96). There are very few examples available of female pilgrims for the period prior to the takeover of Tibet by China. One such pilgrim was the wife of General Zorawar Singh who is said to have lived on the banks of Manasarovar for a couple of years during the early 1840s. However, the first batch of Indian women from Gujarat (barring the Bhotia women who frequently travelled to this region), performed the *parikrama* of Kailash and Manasarovar in the year 1937 (Pranavananda 1949: 226). A portion of Mahatma Gandhi's ashes was immersed in Manasarovar on 8 August 1948 by Mr Surendra and his colleagues.

Many fascinating experiences of people, inspiring both awe and admiration, are associated with trips into western Tibet. Swami Pranavananda performed 36 and 33 *kora*s of Kailash and Manasarovar respectively. His book is a goldmine of information on the Kailash-Manasarovar pilgrimage (*Kailas-Manasarovar*, Calcutta: S.P. League Ltd, 1949). An Indian trader called Purangir went on a pilgrimage to Kailash in 1788 after being given support by the Panchen Lama for ponies, fuel, and servant-cooks at each staging point. He travelled with three attendants and made the usual *parikrama* and took bath in the Manasarovar (Bysack 1890: 99). A sanyasin called Purana Puri, who had chosen the *urdhbahu* (arms raised) attitude for twelve years, performed the pilgrimage to Kailash and Manasarovar during 1770-80 (Duncan 1801: 37-52). In the twentieth century, Sven Hedin of Sweden is perhaps the best known explorer from the West to have explored this region during 1907-09. Entering Tibet via Ladakh, he spent over two months around Manasarovar, sailing on it. He wrote an illuminating account of this region in his books (*Trans-Himalaya: Discoveries and Adventures in Tibet*, 3 vols, London: Macmillan, 1910-1913; *My Life as an Explorer*, reprint, New York: Kodansha International, 1996).

3 Indian Side

I

The Kailash-Manasarovar Pilgrimage done by the Indians traditionally via the 16,400 feet high pass, known as Lipu Lekh, came to a sudden halt in 1959 as a result of sporadic Sino-Indian hostilities. However, after a thaw in the relationship between the two countries, this pilgrimage was allowed again in September 1981. Since then about 450 Indian pilgrims are allowed every year by the Chinese in controlled groups to enter western Tibet directly from India. Besides these pilgrims, local traders from the Kumaon region of Uttarakhand are also allowed to cross the Lipu Lekh Pass with their goods. Border trade is an important source of income for the people of Kumaon. The pilgrims also provide an opportunity to the locals to earn small sums of money by way of porterage and hiring of mules. Though much needs to be done, the facilities along the route are slowly making progress. Kumaon Mandal Vikas Nigam (KMVN) provides food and shelter to pilgrims at highly subsidized rates and the Indo-Tibetan Border Police (ITBP) takes responsibility for their security till the Sino-Indian border. ITBP also provides medical assistance to pilgrims between Gunji and the border. The Government of India has also made provision for evacuation of pilgrims in case of emergency but such facility has been used very rarely. The usually inclement weather makes it almost impossible for a helicopter to land at the designated sites. Once in 1983 the Indian pilgrims were evacuated from Taklakot as the last batch that year had suffered casualties near the Lipu Lekh and some of the passengers could not cross over to the Indian side due to heavy snowfall and blizzards.

The perils faced by pilgrims are many, especially the high altitude, difficult terrain, and unpredictable weather. In earlier times, the problems faced by travellers, who mostly travelled alone, were even worse not only because there were hardly any good means of transport in those days, but also because not much was available by way of accommodation, food, roads, and emergency aid. One traveller towards the beginning of the twentieth century had this to say about his experience:

> Once we missed our way through a forest and had to wander seven days without meeting a single human being, living only on the tender leaves of trees. I thought these things happened

> that I might be trained for the still more arduous labours of my visit to Mount Kailas and lake Manas (Hamsa nd: 50).

The same sadhu writes yet again about another experience:

> One afternoon my old yet strongly built Nepalese guide and myself were passing through a part of the Dehradun forest, merrily chatting and enjoying the luxuriant scenery. On our way through a close green thicket we paused to gaze at a herd of blue monkeys, when suddenly, by instinct, we turned. Bearing down upon us, a wild elephant lumbered not more than twenty yards distant. The elephant had grown lusty, sweat was pouring down his forehead, his trunk uprooting shrubs and throwing them over his wide back. It was the first time that I had seen a wild elephant in the full freedom of nature, and I stood astonished. But my guide was in quite another mood; he saw the danger and only thought of how to escape from it.
>
> Luckily I was brought to myself by the guide's urgent voice, and plunging into the thicket, we lost sight of the beast. We were wending our way again, confidence restored, when there came a rustling sound from a few yards behind us. My guide gave a quick, terrified glance, then cried: 'Swamiji! Run – the elephant is chasing us.' We ran for our lives, the guide in front and myself behind him. A yard or two separated us from the elephant. He was coming after us like an avalanche. In front sank a steep precipice; behind, the elephant, his trunk waving. He was about to pull me down, catching hold of my kafani (sanyasin's gown), and trample me under his feet. We looked at each other – my guide and myself – and then, as one man, threw ourselves down the precipice.
>
> My guide lay unconscious for eleven hours; his legs were bruised green and blue. I was unconscious for a day. I had fallen heavily on my feet. My head felt as though it had sunk down into my waist, and both my waist and legs swelled. But there was no fracture. We sheltered underneath a tree, and my guide treated our injuries with herbs. His legs were cured by a lotion after three days. I took a fortnight for complete recovery (Hamsa nd: 48-49).

Lipu Lekh is crossable only for about four months in a year between the months of June and October. With its demanding but unique itinerary, the pilgrimage through the Indian route offers a variety of unique experiences. Total cost of this pilgrimage comes to about 90,000 INR (about 2,000 USD in 2008).

PER PERSON COST OF THE KAILASH PILGRIMAGE

1. 19,250 INR to be paid to KMVN for boarding and lodging. Out of this amount 5,000 INR is to be deposited as a non-refundable deposit through a demand draft when confirming participation in the pilgrimage (along with indemnity bond, indemnifying the Government of India against any injury or death, during the pilgrimage), and the rest paid on arrival in Delhi before beginning the pilgrimage.
2. 5,000 INR to be paid for health checkup in New Delhi.
3. 400 INR to be paid as collective visa fee at the Chinese embassy.
4. 701 USD to be paid to the Chinese Government at Taklakot.
5. 200 USD for personal expenses in China.
6. 10,000 INR for pony and porter (optional).
7. 10,000 INR collected by most of the Liaison Officers for the common pool for sundry expenses during the pilgrimage.

Every year the first batch of pilgrims leaves in the first week of June and the last batch returns by the first week of October. About 560 pilgrims to be sent in sixteen batches are selected through a lottery out of the thousands who apply. An attempt is made to give each batch a semblance of 'united-in-diversity' India by picking up people from as many states as possible. Out of the 560 pilgrims only about 400 actually manage to begin their pilgrimage as up to 150 persons or so are rejected on various medical grounds by the ITBP doctors in Delhi. The vacancies that fall as a result of this are rarely filled up though Government of India advertises that vacant places are allotted to waitlisted candidates. As medical tests are conducted quite rigorously at Delhi, not many pilgrims nowadays are rejected on medical grounds at Gunji. As there is a huge rush for being included in the list of pilgrims, the Ministry of External Affairs does not allow anyone more than once to go on pilgrimage. But, of course, some people still manage to get around this restriction. For instance, the author met a returning pilgrim between Budhi and Gunji during the 2004 season who told him that it was his fourth trip in a row! The author's trip during 2004 was also his second trip via the Indian route. Keeping in view the Malpa tragedy, each batch of pilgrims is now provided with a satellite phone and other communication gadgets. Now Malpa has actually been taken out of the list of halting points.

A specimen copy of the indemnity bond is sent along with the call letter to each pilgrim. Every pilgrim is required to sign this indemnity bond on a non-judicial stamp paper attested by a First Class Magistrate or notary public. It is mandatory for each pilgrim to deposit it with Government before proceeding on the pilgrimage. One has to declare in this bond that the pilgrimage is undertaken by one at one's own risk. In other words, in case of death or injury, the pilgrim and/or his/her relatives cannot make a claim of any kind against the organizers, i.e., KMVN and Government of India. Thus, no pilgrim is insured for hospitalization, claims, and life. But of course, medical facilities are made available at Dharchula and Gunji. Some medical facilities (basically a first aid box) are also made available at Gala and Budhi. One or two medical personnel are arranged by the KMVN who accompany the pilgrims till Gunji. Beyond Gunji, one doctor and a compounder of the ITBP accompany the pilgrims till Lipu Lekh. Thereafter the pilgrims are on their own. The Chinese have opened a small hospital at Taklakot. Darchen is also supposed to have a hospital but till now it is manned by just one auxiliary nurse.

The pilgrims travel by bus from Delhi to Mangti via Kathgodam, Almora, and Dharchula. The trekking starts from Mangti. The ITBP, Border Roads Organization (BRO), Public Works Department (PWD), KMVN, and officials in the Pithoragarh district administration of Uttarakhand and China Division of the External Affairs Ministry in New Delhi participate in the management of the pilgrimage. The Indian Government keeps a tab on the movement of all groups within India and Tibet and updates the information on its website on a daily basis during the entire season of the pilgrimage. As many members of the Indian Parliament take keen interest in this pilgrimage, Government of India at their behest has been pursuing with the Chinese Government the issue of opening one or two other routes (especially the Ladakh route) for pilgrimage. The Ministry of External Affairs of the Government of India is responsible for the overall control of the pilgrimage which is run by an officer of the rank of Under Secretary. Applications are accepted by the Ministry of External Affairs from mid January till mid April every year. Advertisements inviting applications are placed by Government of India in various newspapers published in different parts of the country.

This is one of the toughest high altitude road journeys on earth and the pilgrims have to be physically fit. Each of the pilgrims is expected in his/her own interest to get a proper advice from one's own doctor to know about one's ability to cope up with the rigours of high altitude trekking in extremely cold and dusty conditions. Keeping this in mind, the medical examination and various tests conducted in Delhi have been made quite comprehensive. As the pilgrimage involves trekking at altitudes of up to 18,500 feet these tests ensure that the intending pilgrims are physically and mentally suitable to endure the rigours of the pilgrimage. Those suffering from high blood pressure, diabetes, asthma, heart disease, epilepsy etc. are rejected outright and are not allowed to undertake the pilgrimage.

The pilgrimage season is also the monsoon season. Though it does not rain much beyond Chiyalekh, sometimes it gets pretty wet between Mangti and Budhi. Water flowing downwards from the hill tops makes use of waterproof coats unavoidable. Moreover, at the higher reaches the weather is quite fickle and the terrain treacherous. During the day the sun is hot and the skin gets tanned very quickly. Unless protective gear and skin-lotion are used, the top-layer of the skin gets burnt within the first two or three days of the trekking. Taking off one's hat immediately after completing the day's trek or wearing it off and on while doing the trekking, gives the worst headache one can imagine! Woollens and wind-cheaters are a must to beat the cold winds. A water bottle, two pairs of trekking shoes with spare laces, at least four pairs each of woollen and cotton socks, a pair of good quality sun glasses, a torch with spare batteries, a large rain coat, water proof pouch for passport and money, a large plastic sheet for water proofing luggage, a Swiss knife, rubber slippers, and a bed-sheet and pillow covers for personal hygiene are advised by the organizers to be carried by each of the pilgrims. On the Indian side, KMVN supplies breakfast, lunch, dinner, and tea (twice) every day. But pilgrims are also advised to carry some extra food by way of dry fruits, biscuits, chocolates, soup powder, etc. But, all these must come within the allowable luggage weight. For any luggage above twenty-five kg an additional fee is levied. Out of this allowance, five kg per person is utilized to carry the collective rations bought by the group for consumption in Tibet. On the Chinese side, food is provided only at Taklakot for four days (first two and last two days of the stay in China). For the remaining nine days, each batch has to carry its own food and cooks. Utensils for cooking are carried into China by the first batch and brought back by the last one. Mostly, the groceries for the Chinese side are donated by an NGO in Delhi. Some provisions can, of course, be bought at Taklakot, Hor Qu, and Darchen. There is no restriction on cameras of any kind. But one has to carry rechargeable batteries of good quality (normal batteries/cells do not work due to high altitude and extreme cold) and a recharger. As discharge rate is faster at higher altitudes, extra rechargeable batteries are an added help. But film rolls and memory sticks used on the Indian side are expected to be deposited at Nabhidhang though this condition is never strictly enforced. Within Tibet there is no restriction on photography except at Taklakot. Of course, the police (almost entirely comprised of Han Chinese) gets quite upset if you take pictures of any building which flies the Chinese flag. Power supply is available for a limited period of time at all the night halts on the Indian side. Within Tibet, Taklakot has a 24-hour supply and Chiu, Trugo, and Dharcen have power supply for a couple of hours every evening. Thus, for the three-day *kora* of Kailash, one must carry sufficient quantity of recharged extra batteries as no facilities for recharging them are available at the night halts of Driraphuk and Zhongzerbu.

The booklet supplied to each pilgrim by the Ministry of External Affairs gives an exhaustive list of not only the various kinds of items to be carried by a pilgrim but also the dos and don'ts to be followed. Those dos and don'ts (including some more helpful ones) are as follows:

1. It is advisable to wear two pairs of socks: a woolen pair and a cotton pair. This is particularly helpful while doing the *kora* of Kailash. A good pair of gloves is also a must. In any case, hands and feet must be protected against extreme cold, as storms occasionally deposit snow on the Kailash circuit, particularly near the Drölma-la.
2. Feet must be kept dry at all times as wet shoes can cause blisters.
3. One must have a wind-cheater in the rucksack and it is helpful to wear more layers of thin clothes than a few thick ones.
4. A sleeping bag is quite desirable as at some of the night halts the quilts and bed-sheets have not been washed ever since they were carted there.
5. A small shoulder bag is very helpful as one can carry most of the essentials in it, particularly a camera and a water bottle.
6. Two pairs of shoes with spare laces must be carried for obvious reasons. It is better to carry shoes which one has already worn for a while. New shoes can sometimes become a source of nuisance for the feet. Shoes must be kept dry and kept inside the sleeping bag if need be.
7. One must wear good sunglasses to protect the eyes.
8. One should avoid trekking alone and should always stay in the company of one or more pilgrims. Getting separated from the group can be extremely risky.
9. Alcohol must be avoided at all cost for the well-being of the body as well as the 'mind.' At high altitudes consumption of alcohol can cause dehydration and disorientation.
10. Trekking should begin as early as possible in the morning as during the afternoon the weather invariably becomes rough.
11. One must never sleep with the boots on.
12. During electric storms one must not point upwards metallic objects such as wireless aerials which can attract lightning. One must also avoid taking shelter under trees and stay away from conical rocks or the top of hills. Open space is safer. One can even sit down on a non-conducting sheet etc., if one has one.
13. Application of sun screen cream or calamine lotion on exposed parts is very helpful to avoid sunburn.
14. One must carry a needle and thread.
15. Drink sufficient quantities of water every day.
16. It is also extremely helpful to bring a bottle of dettol, paper soap, and multi role toilet paper as these are very difficult, if not impossible, to obtain in Tibet.
17. One sometimes loses appetite at high altitudes. But food must not be neglected. Similarly, lose motions sometimes can cause dehydration and thus, sufficient quantities of liquids, especially water, must be drunk daily.
18. It is a good idea to bring some biscuits, chocolate bars, dry fruits, and soup packs. But one must remember to fit all these within the allowable luggage limit.
19. One must never try to make a display of one's bravado.

20. One should not litter on the way. The pilgrimage route on the Indian side has already been affected adversely by pollution caused, besides other things, by plastic bottles, chocolate and chewing gum wrappers, and empty cigarette packets containing silver foil. The author was able to collect over twenty kg of such trash by casually picking up garbage between Lipu Lekh and Mangti while returning in 2004!

II

I received a telegram from the Ministry of External Affairs in May which said that I had been included in the 4th batch. But this was a bit too early for me as I was busy elsewhere. So I asked my friends in government to get me shifted to the 13th batch. And it was done! According to the fixed schedule, pilgrims are called to Delhi batch-wise. Here they are put up at the Gujarat Samaj Bhawan (Rajpur Road) before and after the pilgrimage. For each batch the Indian government appoints a Liaison Officer (LO) who is usually a civil servant. He is issued a satellite phone by the Indian Government which he carries to Tibet for use in emergency. The LO has the authority to act as a 'moral policeman' up to the Indo-Tibetan border and can send a pilgrim back during the onward journey but such a step is rarely taken. The Indian government contributes in terms of infrastructural and material support. A special grant is provided to the ITBP for helping the pilgrims. The ITBP, thus, provides security part of the way, offers welcome receptions during the onward and return journeys, provides snacks and beverages at four or five spots on the way, and pampers pilgrims by providing free group photos. (This may be a means of keeping record of people entering the notified area.) Some of the provincial governments (particularly the governments of Gujarat and Delhi) also provide financial assistance. Being from Delhi, I was lucky to receive 15,000 INR from the Lt. Governor. Now the Government of Delhi has enchanced this subsidy to 30,000 INR. The Delhi Government also gifted to each of the pilgrims a rucksack and waterproof dress.

The pilgrims reach Kathgodam (280 km) by lunch time in a luxury coach. From here they travel by two mini-buses. The first and the second nights of the journey are spent respectively at Almora and Dharchula. Trekking begins from Mangti, which is located at a distance of about 35 km beyond Dharchula. Pilgrims halt for the night after each day's trek at Gala (8 km), Budhi (20 km), Gunji (15 km, two nights), Kalapani (10 km), and Nabhidhang (8 km), reaching Lipu Lekh (7 km) on the ninth day. The ninth night halt is at Taklakot across the border (19 km). KMVN makes all arrangements for accommodation, food, etc. till the border. Pre-fabricated fibre glass huts have now been constructed at all the halting points on the Indian side. Hot water for taking bath and washing clothes can be made available through the porters at Gunji. The LO gets separate accommodation and hot water for bath at all base camps. The toilets at the base camps are tolerable but certainly a luxury compared to their Tibetan counterparts. As generators have been installed at all the base camps, electricity is made available for a few hours for the purpose of charging batteries etc. But one has to compete with the others for recharging batteries as only one or two power outlets are made available. Mattresses and quilts, though not very clean (but certainly better than what one gets in Tibet) are also made available. Ponies and porters for the Indian side of the pilgrimage, depending upon individual requirement, have to be booked at Dharchula and are made available at Mangti for the onward journey and at Lipu Lekh for the return journey. The LO during my previous trip had made hiring of ponies and porters compulsory for everyone, though less than half of the pilgrims were able to use them. His logic was that if you need a pony or a porter midway, how would you have one? All the base camps in India are connected through satellite phones and pilgrims can make calls to anywhere for a nominal fee. A satellite phone for emergency use is also carried by the LO for the duration of the whole pilgrimage.

Before setting off on the pilgrimage, pilgrims have to spend at least three days in Delhi. On the first day in the morning, the pilgrims have to report at the Delhi Heart and Lung Institute (Panchkuian Road, New Delhi) for various tests and have to attend a reception organized by Delhi Government in the afternoon to collect a free rucksack and waterproof gear On the second day, the pilgrims are taken to the Ministry of External Affairs where they are briefed about the pilgrimage. Here they are also shown a documentary film on the Kailash pilgrimage. The indemnity bond signed by the pilgrims is collected. An official of KMVN also collects the remaining 14,250 INR of the 19,250 INR to be paid for making arrangements for 15 days during the *yatra* on the Indian side. Here the LO, who leads the batch, is also introduced. The LO, who is usually an officer of the rank of Under Secretary or above, is appointed by Government of India to facilitate the smooth conduct of the *yatra*. At the time of briefing at the Ministry of External Affairs, passports along with the visa fee are collected by one of the officials. From the Ministry of External Affairs, the pilgrims are taken to a branch of the State Bank of India for collecting Foreign Exchange to be paid to the Chinese Government. Apart from the 701 USD that is to be paid to the Chinese in Taklakot, pilgrims are also allowed to buy a few hundred extra USD for personal expenses, especially for personal shopping and hiring of yaks and porters for the *kora* of Kailash. In the afternoon of the second day, pilgrims are coaxed to attend one or more functions organized by different religious organizations, particularly one called Kailash-Manasarovar Yatra Samiti. This organization offers free rations, *havan samagri* (fuel for the sacrificial fire), and

Kainchi Dham Temple

Temple of Golu Devata

prayer books for the pilgrimage. Though on the first and second day in Delhi one can squeeze in some time for the last minute shopping, the whole of the third day is spent at the ITBP Hospital. Here not only the reports from the Heart and Lung Institute are examined but some additional medical tests are also conducted. At the ITBP Hospital, volunteers from the Amarnath Yatra Samiti offer free lunch and also arrange a couple of lectures to give 'proper guidance' to the pilgrims.

I was rejected by the ITBP doctor as my TMT turned out to be positive. I had not even cared to look at the report when I collected it a day earlier from the Heart and Lung Institute as I had not expected to be declared medically unfit. How could that be? I had already been to Tibet two years ago! I asked the doctor for a second opinion. Reluctantly, he allowed me to go to Batra Hospital which is located across the road from the ITBP Hospital. I had till 1:00 p.m. to come with a fitness certificate. There I paid 500 INR at the counter, got an instant appointment with a doctor on duty, explained to him my situation, and got a fitness certificate. The doctor at the ITBP was satisfied and allowed me to proceed on the *yatra* subject to subsequent clearance at Gunji.

Our batch of 32 pilgrims (25 men and 7 women, including two couples) began its *yatra* on 5 August. We were told to gather at 5:00 a.m. in front of the Gujarat Samaj Bhawan. The KMVN bus was to leave at 5:45 after getting blessings from a couple of sadhus. However, the LO arrived at 6:30 and we could leave only at 6:45. Half a dozen volunteers of the Kailash

Manasarovar Yatra Samiti garlanded the pilgrims and gave each of us a big mounted picture of Mt Kailash, *puja samgri, japamala, bhajan* booklets, religious music cassettes, a packet of camphor, a terrible guide-book written by one Pankaj Kumar Singh, and of course, ample quantities of rations to last the entire journey on the other side of the border. The air-conditioned coach began its journey after a speech by an *acarya* in saffron and hails of *Har Har Mahadeva, Bam Bam Bhole,* and *Om Namah Shivayah.* Some of the pilgrims became quite charged after listening to the speech of the *acarya* and the subsequent slogans. In fact, their sloganeering did not stop till we stopped for lunch at Kathgodam.

After about half an hour we arrived at Ghaziabad. Here we were given a warm farewell by the Ghaziabad All India Manasarovar Committee. A nice but delayed breakfast was offered. All the pilgrims were garlanded and given commemorative medallions. The organizers gave long and quite boring speeches about the good work that the local police boss as well as the MLA had been doing. As I had already heard these speeches during my last trip, I had forewarned the LO about them. So after about 90 minutes he told everybody to board the bus. This upset the organizers very much and some of them in fact said so without mincing words. On the way, we passed through Rampur, Haldwani, Bhawali, and Bhimtal. By the time we reached Kathgodam, the pilgrims had already got 'bonded' into three or four groups. As bigger buses cannot ply in the hills beyond Kathgodam, we got split into two buses here. Our driver had a huge collection of holy songs on Lord Shiva. Some pilgrims had also brought their own cassettes of *bhajans*. All these were played continuously in full volume till we left our bus on the third day of our journey.

The journey till Mangti that we were to complete in a little over two days, used to take over a month in the pre-1959 period. Most of it had to be done on foot besides the fact that some hard core pilgrims would have done it on foot anyway. Wild animals used to be one of the major distractions in those days. One Hindu sadhu who was on his way to Kailash in 1907 writes about one such experience in the Himalayas:

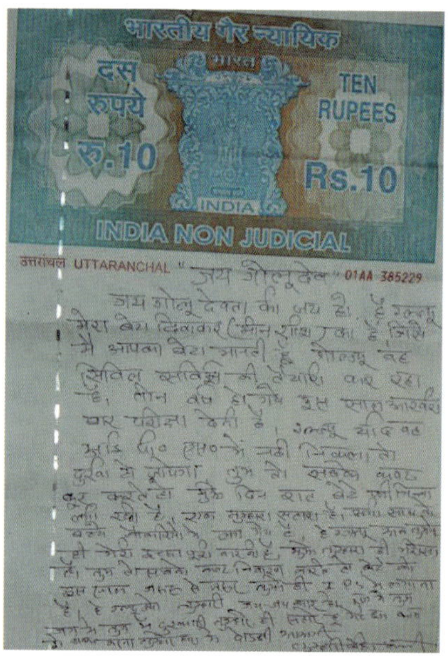

A promise by two warring parties made on a stamp paper to Lord Golu Devata to maintain peace in the future

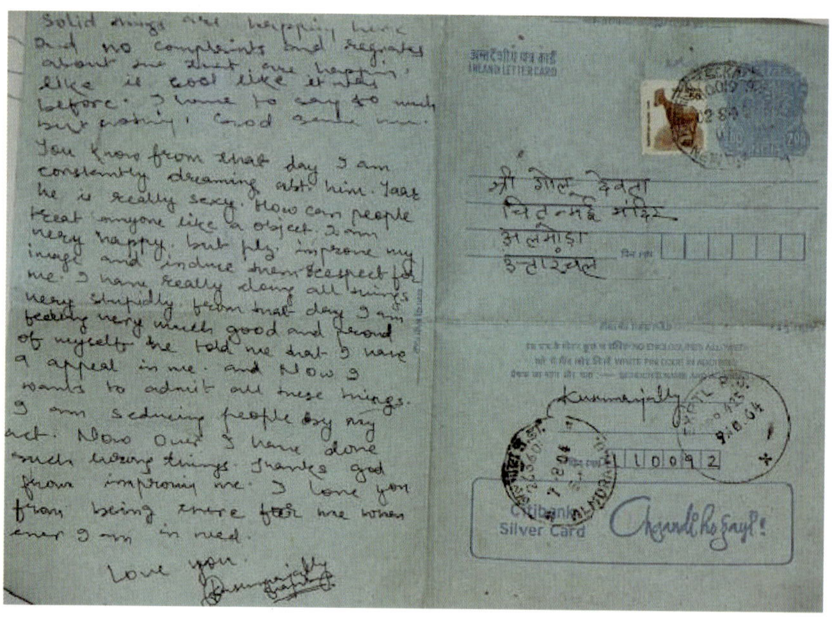

Request made by a woman to Golu Devata for protecting her lover against her husband

Indo-Nepalese border town of Dharchula

> My Nepalese guide and myself . . . had rested for the night at the foot of a tree and spread our blankets and lay down, reclining our heads on the roots as our pillows. Between us we kept burning a log of wood for warmth. I lay down in meditation . . . and soon fell asleep, as I had taken no food and walked the whole day. At about 1 a.m. I awoke suddenly and looked round in the light of our rough hearth . . . . My heart seemed to stop its beating for one awful moment. I sat bolt upright, unable to move. There, stretched out with its tail almost touching my own feet, and its great head facing my coolie, lay a huge tiger. Fascinatedly, I watched its striped, glossy back rise and fall with the cadence of its breathing as, cosily, it warmed itself at our fire . . . . My eyes met those of the coolie. Without moving an inch, he managed to return the message I flashed to him: 'We must not move!' The perspiration oozed from my body. I tried to collect my senses and prepare for the next move of this jungle savage. But at first my brain refused to function. Then, with a tremendous effort of will, I summoned all my powers to think of Shri Sadguru, my Master. Gradually, the panic left me. Even with the tail of the tiger brushing my legs I was able to forget him. A wondrous peace descended over me. While I lay down to rest again, the tiger shambled to its feet, stretched itself, and stood up to its full height – a noble-looking beast. For a while it growled furiously, then lashed its long tail on the ground. Death was very near me then. But I clung to my Master. The tiger smelt round my coolie, then turned its baleful amber eyes towards my feet. For some seconds it paused as if undecided, then jumping over us three or four times, shot away into the thicket . . . . Together we groped our way from the spot through the dark night, and after a mile or two halted, and once more lay down to sleep (Hamsa nd: 67-69).

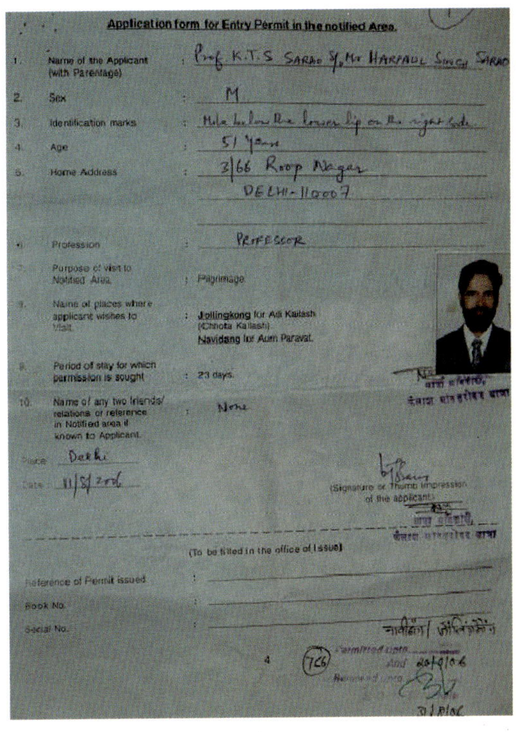

Application form for Entry Permit in the notified Area.

1. Name of the Applicant (with Parentage) : Prof. K.T.S Sarao S/o Mr Harpaul Singh Sarao
2. Sex : M
3. Identification marks : Mole below the lower lip on the right side
4. Age : 51 years
5. Home Address : 3/66 Roop Nagar DELHI-110007
6. Profession : PROFESSOR
7. Purpose of visit to Notified Area : Pilgrimage
8. Name of places where applicant wishes to visit : Jollingkong for Adi Kailash (Chhota Kailash) Navidang for Aum Paravat.
9. Period of stay for which permission is sought : 23 days.
10. Name of any two friends/ relations or reference in Notified area if known to Applicant : None

Place: Delhi
Date: 11/8/2006

(Signature or Thumb Impression of the applicant)

(To be filled in the office of Issue)

Reference of Permit issued :
Book No. :
Serial No. :

4

As the region beyond Dharchula in Uttarakhand is a notified territory, it is out of bounds to foreigners. Indians need a permit to enter this region

The bus from Kathgodam to Almora passes by hundreds of shrines on the way including the famous Kainchi Dham Temple. We reached Almora at 7:00 p.m. and spent our first night of the journey at the tourist guest house of KMVN. The day ended with prayers to Lord Shiva followed by a nice but simple dinner. The older portion of the guest house, where half of the pilgrims spent the night was rather substandard. But the newer portion was very comfortable. Most of the luggage was left on top of the buses as the guest house is located up a hill. So the pilgrims carried only the most essential items with them to the guest house. In fact, this sorting out had already been done at Kathgodam as per instructions from the accompanying KMVN guide.

On the second day, all got up at 4:30 a.m. After a quick cup of tea, we assembled for a prayer to start the day's journey and off we went in the two buses with chants of *Om Namah Shivayah*. About eight kilometres from Almora, we stopped for about 30 minutes at the temple of Lord Goludev (some local maps show it as Gaulu Devata) at Chitai. Here can be seen hundreds of small and big bells tied to all available spots by devotees within the premises of the temples. These devotees either come in person from all over north India with their written appeals or send them by post to the deity of this temple. These appeals to the deity are written on various kinds of material including stamp paper, inland letters, postcards, greeting cards, and sheets of plain paper and are hung in the sanctum sanctorum as and when they arrive. In these appeals devotees make requests, prayers, or promises to the deity for assistance, protection, or to be a witness. Thus, there was a letter by a woman praying for the protection of her lover as well as herself against her husband. There was an undertaking written on a stamp paper relating to a land dispute between two parties swearing in the name of Lord Goludev that they shall abide by the terms of

Pilgrims have to frequently face landslides and tread through difficult terrain

Trekking from Mangti till Kalapani is along the banks of Kali which forms border between India and Nepal

the agreement. A letter by a woman sought Lord Goludev's intervention so that she could get married to her lover who belonged to a caste different from hers. There was another letter in which an unemployed young woman implores the deity to help her in getting a job. Over half a dozen letters from students consisted of appeals for good marks in an examination.

We stopped for breakfast at Dhol. Lunch was provided at the KMVN guest house at Chakori. With its beautiful log huts, Chakori is an ideal place if one is looking for a quiet and romantic place. We reached Mirthi at 2:00 p.m. where the ITBP had made arrangements for our welcome.

A Bhotia Temple

Zhebu/Jhibbu

After a group photo and some refreshment, we continued our journey towards the town of Dharchula where we arrived at 5:00 p.m. We spent our second night here at the KMVN guest house. This place is believed to have received its name after the Pandavas set up a gigantic oven (*chulha*) in the hill to cook food en route to Kailash. This town is located on either side of the river Kalinadi which forms the border between India and Nepal. Nepalese and Indians are allowed to move freely across the narrow footbridge guarded by the security forces of the two countries on their respective sides. However, the gates of the bridge are closed between 6:00 p.m. and 6:00 a.m. due to the menace of Marxist guerrillas on the Nepalese side. Writing about this town in 1906, the Commissioner of the area says that Dharchula at that time was 'the winter headquarters

Restaurant run by a Bhotia family between Gala and Budhi

Bhotias sacrificing a goat at Garbyang

A Bhotia trader bringing a consignment of wool from Tibet

of the Political Peshkar, the residence of two missionary ladies, and the cold weather rendezvous of very large number of Bhotias; while on the Nepalese side there . . . (was) . . . a court house, a gaol and the residence of the Nepalese Lieutenant, who . . . (was) . . . in civil and criminal charge of this part of the country. The bridge connecting the two sides here . . . (was) . . . composed of one rope!' (Sherring 1906: 21-22). In the view of Bhagwan Shri Hamsa, in summer 'Darachula is uncomfortably hot, and consequently flies are numerous' (Hamsa nd: 81-82).

Almost immediately after our arrival at the Dharchula guest house various formalities regarding the trekking, weighing of luggage, and hiring of ponies and porters were completed. Already over a hundred young and old men had gathered in the premises of the guest house. They all had ID cards issued by the local authority and were beseeching all the pilgrims to hire them and/or their ponies. The hostel manager warned us against hiring anybody directly as many of them were not 'reliable'. Later, my porters told me that the manager actually got a cut from the porters and pony herders who were hired through him. These ponies and porters accompany the pilgrims till the Indo-Tibetan border. Fortunately, the LO did not make it mandatory for all pilgrims to hire porters and ponies. Thus, I decided not to hire any. Then suddenly, Harak Singh, my porter of last journey, came over to me and told me that this season he had not been hired as yet. He was a good guy and had excellent knowledge of the local geography and folklore. So I hired him to

Like the Tibetans, sometimes the Bhotias use sheep and goats to transport goods

A guest being welcomed at a Bhotia wedding

carry my water bottle, camera, and a few other little things.

The people of Uttarakhand living closer to the border are known as Bhutia or Bhotia and they call the Tibetans as Hunia. The people lower down are a mixture of Nepalese, Bhotias, and local Kumaonis. Majority of them do farming and breed livestock. During the winter nearly all of them abandon their villages and move to Dharchula. 'Bhotias . . . intrepid traders as they are, yearly endure vicissitudes of climate and dangers of mountaineering which win our admiration for their manly qualities' (Sherring 1906: 4). The Bhotias have preserved their heritage assiduously and are always ready to show glimpses of it through their dance and music. They speak a mixture of Hindi and Tibetan. Though the Bhotias call themselves Hindu and 'Singh' is the middle name of most of them, they follow many customs and ceremonies that are very similar to the people of western Tibet. Some of them eat beef, have chörtens, mani-walls, stone cairns, and flag poles. Some of them even dress up like the Tibetans. Towards the beginning of the twentieth century, their disposal of the dead also used to have many similarities with the Tibetan practice. For instance, a visitor in 1907 observed:

> At Rung, a nearby village, a Bhutia had died that day, and here I was given the opportunity of witnessing the ceremony of the last sacrament practised among these people. It was a strange affair, too. The dead body is hacked into pieces, tied in a bundle and placed on a bier which is carried in a musical procession, comprising both men and women, to the place for cremation. Every family must bring fuel to the consuming fire (Hamsa nd: 86-87).

But such practices are slowly giving way to the *samskaras* of mainstream Hinduism. With the advent of tourism into the region and the arrival of all those things that go with tourism,

Bhotia women

Bhotia children

what the Commissioner of the region wrote in 1906 about these people does not appear to be true any more:

> They are extremely particular as to the water they drink, never drinking from anywhere except at the actual source of the spring, and all river water they refuse absolutely, fearing contamination. They do not carry these sanitary precautions as far as their dwelling houses, for the smell

A typical Bhotia house

Bhotia houses have elaborately carved doors and windows

Ganpati adorns the entry to a typical Bhotia house

> round their abodes is simply appalling, and in person these aborigines look as if they had never washed in their lives. They live in stone houses, nicely built, and have a few fields of cultivation adjoining (Sherring 1906: 17).

The women in the Kumaon region, according to Sherring, 'laugh at everything and everybody, and do not rush away to hide, or draw their veils over their faces as the Southerners' (Sherring 1906: 56). Talking about an encounter with young Bhotia women in 1907, a sadhu writes:

> I was seated alone in the open, meditating to myself, the snow-capped mountains gleaming before me, when a group of four or five young girls came running towards me, whispering to one another in their strange language. I was preoccupied, and in no mood to be disturbed. I thought, if I ignored them, they would go away. Instead, they began to laugh aloud, and I might never have discovered the reason of these painful attentions had not the schoolmaster, who had overheard their conversation, come to my assistance and explained that the girls had taken a fancy for me and wished me to prolong my stay . . . . I retired hastily inside, and later the schoolmaster told me that in this part of the country young girls, and grown-up women also, mixed freely with men, but that seldom was evil meant. He tried to persuade me to let the girls sing and dance for us, but I being adverse to his proposal, the matter was dropped (Hamsa nd: 87-88).

According to Sherring, amongst the Bhotias, who are divided into two castes i.e., Rajputs (upper class) and Dumras (lower caste) (Sherring 1906: 65):

> there are many men and women who are unmarried, and a rich man, though ever so desirous of wedlock, has often been known to go wifeless, because of an offending eye, or a nose which was not acceptable. The Bhotia maid has to be wooed and won, and if her heart is not in the arrangement, no marriage takes place. Such is the race of Bhotias who have for centuries fought with the inclemency of the weather, conquered all difficulties of the road, and mastered the loftiest and most perilous passes (Sherring 1906: 73) . . . . (they) . . . arrange marriages at the rambang, which is the village club, and generally a very disreputable place . . . . Girls start to go to the rambang from the age of ten years, and practically never sleep at home after that age, the result being that a virtuous girl is scarcely known . . . . As is to be expected, a system such as this leads to the freest intimacy, and one sees a man walking about with his arm round a girl's waist (Sherring 1906: 104).

Bhagwan Shri Hamsa, observed in 1907 that the Bhotias 'are cruel by nature; singing and dancing are their chief amusements. Young people of both sexes, married or single, mix freely with each other in sport, merriment and dance. Women manage the homes and fields, while men look to trades' (Hamsa nd: 67).

On the third day, we left at 8:00 a.m. Our buses were to take us to Mangti located at a distance of 35 km from Dharchula. Entry into this region is subject to a special permit issued by the District Collector. Non-Indians are completely prohibited from entering this area. After we moved halfway to Mangti, there had been a landslide. So we had to abandon the buses and cross over to the other side on foot. We managed to hire four jeeps and reached Mangti without losing much time. Ponies and porters were already waiting for us there. We began our trekking after crossing the bridge built on the Mangti creek. The first half of the trekking was a paved road going uphill. The second half was a foot passage. This eight-km trek to Gala was quite pleasant except that two incidents of the previous trip came constantly to my mind. Here, at one of the natural fountains, I decided to fill up my flask with fresh water. After having filled it up, I realized that a few metres above me the water had actually been flowing through horse droppings! One has to be very careful while collecting drinking water in these mountains and make sure that water is flowing down from a place which has not been frequented by horses and ponies. The second incident had long term consequences. When we began our trekking from Mangti, the LO 'ordered' me to walk with him (which I did throughout the pilgrimage). And he decided to walk at the end of the trail. Most of the pilgrims who were walking were in front followed by ponies and the two of us at the rear. These ponies were releasing so much foul gas that trekking became a nightmare! I told Sudhir to at least let the ponies be behind us. But he would hear nothing of it!

Everybody reached Gala (7,950 feet) by 2:00 p.m. It rained most of the night. The roof of my hut was leaking. The mattresses spread on the floor were quite damp. My hut also did not

Landscape: Gala to Budhi

Many social and religious practices of the Bhotias resemble the Tibetans. They raise stone cairns, build chortens, and put heads of dead animals at important spots to keep away the evil spirits

Flora in the Bhotia region

ITBP checkpost shortly after Garbyang

Landscape: Garbyang to Gunji

have any toilet. So one had to use the one located near the door of another hut situated some fifty feet behind. Walking to this toilet in dark was a bit unnerving considering that the Gala camp is located on an uneven hillside. I did not get much sleep at night.

On the fourth day, we began our twenty-four km trek to Budhi (8,350 feet) at about five in the morning. The trek from Gala to Malpa had become very slippery due to incessant rain. My polythene raincoat (bought in Taiwan for the equivalent of 12 INR) was not very helpful as the strong winds brought in so much water that by the time we reached Malpa, I was drenched to the skin. The whole path is narrow and pebbly, interspersed with steep ascents and sudden descents. I was reminded of Shri Hamsa's observation: 'This part of the journey is formidably difficult for Bhutia tradesmen, their mules, horses, goats and goods often slipping off the narrow path to plunge deep down into the valley to inevitable doom' (Hamsa nd: 50). The first seven to eight

Kalinadi between Gala and Budhi

Nagphali, also known as Cobra fruit, results in swelling if its sap touches any part of the body

km of the trek were largely a downward journey consisting of 4,400 steps made in stony ground. After descending these steps we reached Lakhanpur. We had our breakfast here. Hereafter the path follows the right bank of the river Kali. The sound of the gushing water is extremely loud and musical. We had to cross a number of waterfalls. Waterfalls on the way were spectacular. Water falling from an altitude looks like milk. Some of the scenes are breath-taking, especially when light passes through the thin layers of water coming down from the mountains.

The mountains at Malpa (7,200 feet), located about fifteen km from Gala, loom around like massive forts. Earlier there used to be a night halt at Malpa. But the base camp here was closed after more than 300 people including 40 pilgrims perished in a major landslide on 17 August 1998. Among them was Protima Bedi. She is learnt to have once said, 'When I die, don't put me in those metal incinerators.' Probably, she was granted death the way she wanted so that her remains could become part of the grand Mother Earth. Now two or three teashops have been built here above the mound hundreds of feet underneath which the pilgrims lie buried. The pilgrims these days just stop here to have a quick lunch at a small restaurant and then march

Landscape: Budhi to Gunji

The Sinking village of Gargyang

ahead. Budhi is a small village with about ten two-storeyed houses which have carved doors and windows.

The twenty-four kilometre trek to Gunji (11,700 feet) begins with a steep climb to Chiyalekh (12,200 feet). On the other side of Chiyalekh lies the beautiful small plateau called Chhetothanga. Here the ITBP camp offers tea and refreshments to the pilgrims. Chhetothanga has abundance of flowers of various colours and butterflies. After Chiyalekh the trail becomes fairly smooth and less wet. Yaks can inhabit in Uttarakhand only between Chiyalekh and the border. The height prior to Chiyalekh is too low. This makes the air too dense and the temperature too high for the yaks to survive. Though yak is a great beast of burden it is not so disciplined and cannot be used in tilling the soil. But *jhibbu*, a cross between a cow and a yak, can survive almost everywhere and is much more docile than a yak. Thus, the people in this area prefer a *jhibbu* to a yak. Between Chiyalekh and Gunji is located the famous sinking village of Garbyang (10,000 feet). Though we had managed to reach the village of Garbyang by about 11: a.m. on the fifth day from Delhi, in the good old days it used to take 'nearly two months to reach Garbyang from Kathgodam, the way being through hills, dales, forests and across rivers' (Hamsa nd: 97). As we were entering Garbyang, a little below us the villagers could be seen sacrificing a goat in their temple. A family was celebrating the first-time visit of a son-in-law.

At a short distance from Garbyang, a wooden bridge called Sitapul exists for crossing over into Nepal. But the adjacent Nepalese territory is under the control of Maoists who have put up their red flag. Sometimes the Maoist guerrillas can actually be seen guarding the approach to the bridge. Down below the village is the confluence of Kalinadi and Tinkar. From Garbyang can be seen the Nepalese village called Chhangru located on top of a hill beyond a flat expanse of land. A different route to reach Tibet is in existence via Chhangru in Nepalese territory. Apparently Nepalese do not need a visa to go on the Kailash pilgrimage and the Chinese allow them even if they show a bona fide letter from a village panchayat. Some Indians sadhus are also said to use this route but the Maoist guerrillas have to be paid for passing through as they control most of this region.

Except for a short stretch, the trail between Budhi and Gunji is along the Kalinadi. At a short distance from Garbyang, ITBP has set up a check post to scrutinize the documents and register the people passing through. No one can pass through here without showing authorization papers and an ID card. From here onwards, one also begins to see bare tops of mountains. Some very unique and beautiful rock formations can be seen on the way. The mountains are full of pine, deodar (Himalayan cedar), and *bhojapatra* trees. The area of Napalchu and Gunji villages starts with fields, huts and halting sheds. Gunji is the junction of two valleys, Kutighati and Lipughati. The pilgrims spend two nights at Gunji (11,700 feet).

Gunji village as seen from Napalchu

Confluence of Kalinadi and Kutinadi at Gunji

The sixth day was a day of rest at Gunji. The final medical examination is done by the ITBP doctors at Gunji. These doctors specialize in high altitude medicine. During the pilgrimage season, a doctor is specifically posted here to accompany each batch of pilgrims till the border and escort them back safely. Those pilgrims whom the doctor considers unfit are not allowed to travel beyond Gunji. Both the times I was cleared without any hitch. During both of my trips, half a dozen pilgrims in each batch were told to appear twice before the medical team. This naturally makes the pilgrims a bit more religious for the day. As by this time, bonding between pilgrims takes place fairly strongly, no one wants anybody to be left behind. As a matter of fact, a pilgrim is rarely stopped here as almost all the doubtful cases are weeded out in Delhi itself. During my first visit, as the LO was one of the six persons to be initially held on medical grounds, it gave a bit of scare to everybody. So his clearance in the evening made everybody very happy. But Lakshmi seemed the happiest of all as she claimed that her prayers at the nearby Shiva temple actually enabled the LO to finally clear the medical obstacle. The LO too declared that Lakshmi's songs in her melodious voice sung at the temple were responsible for winning Lord Shiva to his side.

Gunji village, located on the left bank of Kuti river has about eighty double-storey houses. Napalchu hamlet located across the bridge from Gunji has another ten houses. A total of about 350 people live in these two settlements. There are about half a dozen shops in Gunji and none in Napalchu. But as goods have to be transported here on ponies either from Dharchula or Taklakot in summer, they are quite expensive. For instance, onions were being sold at 60 INR a kilo. The squalid houses of Gunji are adorned with innumerable poles supporting little flags with or without prayers and pious phrases written on them. One can also see some stone cairns in and around the village just like in Tibet. The Gunji camp is the most spacious amongst all the base camps. Indian Customs and Excise Department as well as State Bank of India have put up their branches in the neighbourhood of the camp. A sub-divisional magistrate also functions from here. But all of them have to close shop during winter. The Public Works Department has also built a guest house. The ITBP camp here has its own TV room and some other recreational activities which they gladly share with the pilgrims. It was a great feeling to hear news on the TV after a gap of several days. In the evening, all of us were invited by the Commanding Officer over tea and a friendly volleyball match with the jawans. The day ended with a prayer in the small Shiva temple manned by the ITBP personnel. Uttaranchal Police relinquish charge of the pilgrims here to the ITBP personnel.

The nine-kilometre trek on the seventh day from Gunji to Kalapani (11,880 ft) was the easiest so far. From here onwards armed guards of the ITBP accompany the pilgrims and stay with them till they cross over to the Tibetan side. Pilgrims are huddled together and are covered by the guards at the rear and the front. As the entire pilgrimage route from Dharchula till the border is alongside the Indo-Tibetan border and the Nepalese side is controlled by the Maoist guerrillas, the pilgrims are protected by the ITBP in a businesslike manner. A few days prior to our arrival in the area, some Indian merchants had been kidnapped by these guerrillas. The ITBP jawans therefore were taking no chances. Whenever anyone was a little slow and lagged behind, they would simply stop the entire group till all were together. The whole trek is accompanied by breath-taking scenery. The journey took about four hours of an extremely leisurely and pleasant walk. The pilgrimage trail is on the right bank of Kalinadi, but Kalapani base camp is located on the left side of the river. This was the first time that we crossed Kalinadi on to its left side. Originally, Kalapani was Nepalese territory which was leased from Nepal in exchange for a place called Mahindergarh. A few years back some Nepalese, in fact, had made an attempt to take over

Landscape: Gunji to Kalapani. Kalinadi which forms border between India and Napal is much sober and smaller here

The Village Meeting-Place at Gunji

Site of a new bridge at Gunji

the Kalapani camp. But they chickened out on realizing that the well-armed ITBP guys were not in a mood to oblige them. The river Kali basically makes its debut from here. 'The pilgrim, passing through the country of the Bhotias, viz., Chaudans and Byans, he is to worship, at Kalapani, the springs, which the devout Hindu considers the source of the river Kali, and most sacred to the goddess of that name' (Sherring 1906: 50). There is a small temple with idols of both Shiva and Kali. Inside the sanctum sanctorum, we were all ushered in one by one to be shown in a small chamber the Kalinadi originating! This small temple with a large courtyard is designed beautifully. Two passages leading to the temple are decorated with hundreds of small bells tied on plastic ropes on either side. These bells make nice sound in the breeze or whenever

Golden Peak Nagphani at Kalapani

Landscape: Kalapani to Nabhidhang

Wreck of a crashed helicopter at Nabhidhang

one of the ropes is pulled. As in the Gunji temple soldiers join the pilgrims in the evening prayers and *bhajan* singing at the temple.

Near the Kalapani camp is a sulphur geyser where rudimentary arrangements are available for a bath. There is a cave, known as the Vyas Asram, which is located about 500 feet directly above in the hill. A flag hoisted by the ITBP soldiers at the door of the cave can be seen from the base camp. The legend has it that Vyas wrote the epic *Mahabharata* in this cave. In this region, dotted all over the hill sites are various temples dedicated to this saint revered by folks in this area. The Pandava brothers are said to have passed through this area on their way to Kailash and according to one of the legends, thirsty Arjuna shot an arrow into the ground from where sprang forth water. The jawans here produce their own electricity through a small hydro-electric generator. It was installed by one of the ITBP officers. Passports are checked and stamped here by officials of the Immigration Department. They maintain a

One of these two temples was built by the survivors of a helicopter crash at Nabhidhang

Om Parvat in 2007

register here with records of all those who pass through here in either direction. Small creeks flowing into Kalinadi from the Nepalese side make the whole area look very serene. The night at Kalapani was very cold. The poor porters slept in a derelict hut with almost no protection. One pilgrim had very acute headache. At high altitudes cold winds blow and if one does not keep one's head covered at all times while trekking, one is bound to get a headache. As a matter of fact, the headache is quite unnerving and keeps bothering for about two days. Only after I got it myself did I realize that the ITBP doctor was not joking when he had told us in Delhi to take precautions against such a possibility.

The nine-km trek on the eighth day from Kalapani to Nabhidhang (13,880 ft) was completed in a very leisurely trek of about four hours. Kalapani and Nabhidhang do not have any human settlements except that the ITBP soldiers and a few other government officials camp here during the summer. So far no one seemed to have any breathing problem or suffered from AMS (acute mountain sickness, also known as 'mountain sickness'). On the way, ITBP provided tea and nice snacks. The weather at Nabhidhang became quite bad in the afternoon. It was raining the whole day and went on pouring till past midnight. At Nabhidhang, the famous Om Parvat can be seen on a clear day. Permanent snow in the natural curves on top of the black rock face makes the

---

Preceding pages: Nabhi of Goddess Gauri at Nabhidhang

symbol of *Om*. Since it was quite cloudy, the symbol could not be seen. Nabhidhang being the last camp on the Indian side, all the exposed film rolls including the one in the camera need to be deposited with the ITBP authorities here. The rolls are given back to the pilgrims when they pass by here on their return journey.

The ninth day was the toughest day thus far. After saying prayers and singing the National Anthem (after all, the border was close by!), our journey began at sharp 2 a.m. Bournvita and cornflakes were served for breakfast. We were expected to reach the top of Lipu Lekh (16,400 ft) before sunrise where we would meet the returning batch. A Tibetan guide would receive us at the border and escort us to Taklakot. The ITBP doctor and the armed escorts would return along with the returning batch of pilgrims who would rendezvous with us at the border. It was pitch dark, extremely cold, and drizzly. We had to grope our way with the help of torches. The ITBP soldiers were helpful and escorted the procession from the front as well as the rear. Once in a while the drizzle was turning into snow. The laboured breathing of the ponies and the clatter of their hooves on the stones gave somewhat of an eerie effect to the procession. The trekking was certainly arduous considering that once in a while one had to wade through poodles of extremely cold water. A couple of dogs kept by the ITBP soldiers were also giving us company. Breathing was a bit difficult considering that it was cold and the atmosphere rarefied. Some of the pilgrims were inhaling camphor again and again. In fact, a couple of them had tied it to their wrists like watches so that every now and then they could just rub the same on the tips of their frozen noses. Three people had to be revived with oxygen. All except five pilgrims were riding ponies. About halfway through, the first traces of dawn began to appear and silhouettes of people and ponies could be seen. Outlines of the mountain peaks against the crimson sky made the occasion a very

Om Parvat in 2002

sombre one indeed! By 7:30 a.m. we made it to the top. The returning batch also arrived at about the same time. We greeted each other shouting *Kailash Pati ki Jai, Bharat Mata ki Jai.* (It was the border, so the Chinese must hear it! But, of course, there were only Tibetans with their ponies.) During the 1962 hostilities, Chinese horsemen are said to have advanced till the border but returned without advancing further. It is said that the Indian Government gave up the idea of building a road till the border due to reasons of tactical disadvantage. Our luggage was shifted to Tibetan ponies. The exchange of pilgrims and other formalities between the two Tibetan guides and the ITBP personnel were completed in about half an hour. After this we began our onward journey towards Taklakot.

4 Lipu Lekh to Darchen

We were met by two Tibetan 'guides' at the border who escorted us to Taklakot (12,800 ft). The cross over into Tibet was quite unusual and certainly different from all the other land-crossings between India and neighbouring countries which I had gone across. I remember having crossed into Pakistan through the Attari-Wagah crossing in 2001 and 2006 and to Myanmar through the Tammu-Moreh crossing in 2005. Both times at Attari-Wagah it had taken more than 14 hours to clear immigration and customs formalities. There were a large number of armed paramilitary personnel riding horses who guided the train across no-man's land. The Tammu-Moreh crossing, where the locals are allowed to go across the border for a day's shopping by paying ten rupees each, too had taken an entire day. At both the crossings harassment by the immigration and customs officials was endless. But at the Lipu Lekh crossing, there was virtually no one from the customs or immigration departments of the two countries. The Indian immigration authorities had checked our passports two days earlier and twenty kilometres before the border. On the Chinese side our passports were checked at Taklakot which is another twenty kilometres beyond the border. For the record, if not anything else, Chinese immigration officials did not even stamp our passports.

It would not be easy for anyone to cross Lipu Lekh unnoticed. The pass can only be crossed during about four months in the summer and the narrow passage that passes through the immigration barracks at Kalapani is unavoidable. Of course, the dogs would make it impossible for anything strange to pass unnoticed through Kalapani. Once in a while Tibetans are known to have tried to cross over to the Indian side through this pass. They are almost certainly caught at Kalapani, if not at Nabhidhang before that. After being interrogated, they are invariably pushed back and left at the mercy of by the Chinese authorities.

Water in the little creeks begins to flow towards Tibet beyond the Lipu Lekh whereas before the border it flows southwards into India. This seems to make it look like a natural border. Landscape also changes completely. Land becomes more levelled and less rocky on the Tibetan side. In fact, the Chinese have been able to build a jeepable road right up to the border. As per the treaty between India and China, some locals are issued special ID cards and are allowed free entry

View of Tibet from Lipu Lekh

into Tibet for trading in local goods and to assist pilgrims. Thus, on the way one comes across caravans of ponies carrying loads of wool, electronic goods, and rock-salt towards India and jaggery and rice towards Tibet.

Pilgrimage via the Lipu Lekh has become much easier and safer after it was reopened in 1981. In the pre-1959 period pilgrimage to Tibet was largely an unregulated affair. But now it has become a much more controlled venture on both sides of the border. Prior to 1959, only sadhus used to venture into Tibet. Lay pilgrims almost completely avoided Tibet unless they got permission from the Tibetan authorities to carry weapons and manpower to defend themselves against the bandits. These bandits invariably used to waylay unarmed pilgrims and traders. On the Indian side, KMVN has built base camps all along the way where pilgrims are provided proper meals, shelter, communication facilities, and security. In Tibet, the Chinese government provides accommodation, guides, and transport for the entire pilgrimage. Pilgrims are also provided Chinese vegetarian food at Taklakot.

Our ponies and porters turned back from the border but we were allowed to carry four Indian cooks with us. The downward trek of about six km beyond the Lipu Lekh crossing was easy. By about 11:00 a.m. (Chinese standard time is two and a half hours ahead of the Indian Standard Time), all pilgrims had made it to the base of the mountain. About half of the pilgrims rode ponies, some of them doing so because they did not have to pay for them. The charges for these ponies are included in the USD 701 which each of the pilgrims has to pay to the Chinese. A 40-seater bus which had brought the returning pilgrims was waiting. Our luggage also arrived at about the same time and was loaded on to the bus almost immediately.

Purang Guest House at Taklakot

The first view of Tibet from the Lipu Lekh is magnificent and the primeval beauty of the landscape is incomparable. As pointed out by Sherring, 'the impression on the beholder is that the scene before him is truly one of nature's grandest handiworks. There is no tree or verdure to relieve the severity of what he sees, and the almost total absence of animal life adds to the feeling of intense desolation prevalent everywhere' (Sherring 1906: 166). The landscape provided a rare glimpse of barren rock and Tibetan desert. Rock formations are extremely beautiful and unique. Various colours of these rocks, especially the unique patterns created by the falling sunlight, give the landscape a very special appearance. It is almost impossible to see any vegetation on the mountains. As we realized during our stay, Tibet is dotted with some of the greatest and awe-inspiring marvels in the world. The route is surrounded by high mountain ranges, the highest being the Gurla Mandhatta (23,350 feet).

The Chinese Market at Taklakot

About eight kilometres down from the border, near the village of Pala, was a small check post manned by about half a dozen military personnel. At the time of Sherring's visit, it was 'a Tibetan outpost, the garrison being composed of one watchman, who . . . [was] more conspicuous by his absence than his presence. There . . . [was] accommodation for travellers in the shape of two rest-houses, built to face north as a protection from the prevailing south wind' (Sherring 1906: 167). On the way to Taklakot, we passed through Magrum village located by the side of the Karnali river (Map Chu). The village consists of about twenty mud houses some of which are in a poor and dilapidated condition. Closer to Taklakot, there are small patches of land growing wheat, rice, maize, barley, and chick peas. Irrigation and harvesting techniques and use of machinery appeared to be suitable considering the geography. We reached the Pulin Guest House at Taklakot (known as Purang and Pulin in Tibetan and Chinese respectively) shortly before 2:00 p.m. However, in the pre-1959 days, the 20-km trek from Lipu Lekh to Taklakot was not so easy. Bhagwan Shri Hamsa talking about his experience towards the beginning of the twentieth century points out:

> Though Taklakot seemed so near, yet we could not reach the place before 7.30 p.m. We travelled continuously for fifteen hours this day. On reaching Taklakot we found the river Karnali was flooded. Nor was there a bridge. We had to cross the river on the backs of animals. On the opposite bank was a big cave carved out in the rock with several Gumphas (rooms) in it. I stayed in one of these rooms for the night, after having it swept clean of the accumulated refuse. My friend the Bhutia merchant put up in another Gumpha after unloading the animals, for they were to be sent back to Tinker that very night, no fodder being available for them at Taklakot... Here we met with half a dozen Tibetans. They were dead drunk. Working their ogre faces, they threatened to kill us if we did not immediately leave Tibetan territory. They posed as Tibetan officers. When we did not move, they grew turbulent. It was 8.30 p.m. I

The Gokung Gompa and ruins of the Shimbiling Gompa and the Dzongpon could not understand a word of what they said. The Bhutia trader, however, explained something to them, and they went away for a time. The Tibetans are a wild people, and a foreign traveller is likely to feel in constant dread of his life amongst them (Hamsa nd: 108-109).

He writes further:

Parma Bhutia came to us and introduced an old Sadhu who accompanied him... I learnt from the Bhutia that the old Sadhu was no other than Morpankhi Bawa, who had been making

Outskirts of Taklakot

Landscape: Taklakot to Darchen

annual pilgrimage from Muttra to Kailas for the last twelve years... It was the Bawa's vow to visit annually Kailas-Manas for one Tapa (twelve years), and to spend each year a month and a half at Kailas in meditation of Lord Siva. This was his twelfth year, and Morpankhi Bawa was returning from his last visit to Kailas-Manas... he used to travel sixty miles every day, and could go from Durchin to Taklakot in a single day. He had gone to Kailas only a couple of months before me, at a time when the whole of Lipu pass is frozen with ice, and even goats find it hard to cross. Some years back he used to wear a cap with peacock feathers, and so was called Morpankhi Bawa... He was reputed... to have a good knowledge of herbs and drugs (Hamsa nd: 119-120).

The Purang Guest House has eight independent units in a row each consisting of a big room and a small anteroom with seven beds in each unit. The shower rooms were opened daily for about an hour. The toilet block was particularly noxious consisting of cemented pits in a row joined by a channel in the middle. There were no doors. But the men's and women's areas were separated by a wall. One of the girls flushed the toilet block with a hosepipe once a day. It would be unwise to enter this place after sunset, at least not without a torch and a mask. In any case, one is always in for a surprise in Tibet. I was attacked by one of the roosters hiding in the bushes near the toilet block! Its beak was powerful enough to draw blood from my leg.

Hot water flasks were supplied in all the rooms. The vegetarian food included unlimited quantities of boiled rice, vegetables cooked in the Chinese style, and canned fruit. Two days in Taklakot gave us the taste of a forgotten civilization. Taklakot has restaurants, shops, and a post office. We were told by the guides to wait for the Chinese officials to get our passports and group visa checked. We were not allowed to venture out of the guesthouse till our documents had been checked and payment for the trip made. The officials arrived only in the evening and thus a whole day was wasted. During my visit in 2004, the checking of passports was done in the rudest possible way. The young official sat with his feet on the table, drinking Lhasa beer and smoking cheap quality cigarettes. Pilgrims were called by his assistant to stand up before him one by one. The poor English of the official made things quite awkward for those pilgrims who themselves could not speak much of it. Intervention by others to help only invited severe rebukes. The moment the immigration official saw Taiwanese visa in my passport, he grew quite furious, threw my passport in a corner, and started shouting abuse in Chinese. It took quite some time for his temper to cool down. Three pilgrims were threatened with deportation because they had gone out of the guest house before getting their passports checked. In fact, they were arrested taking pictures of a Chinese flag. Though they were allowed to go, their cameras were released only the next day in the evening. The 'guides' were also scolded severely for not having kept us confined to the guesthouse.

Taklakot is the administrative centre (*xian*) of the Purang county of Ali district. All tourists must register on arrival in this town. The office of the Public Security Bureau is located opposite the Peacock Hotel. There is a bank, a telecom office, and two markets (Nepalese [Dharchula Bazar] and Tibetan) besides the main market on either side of the road. A few private shops now have an ISD facility. Taklakot is located on the Karnali river which flows from here to Nepal. With a population of around 12,000 it is the biggest settlement in western Tibet. It is also the furthermost outpost of Chinese officialdom in Tibet. There is a military base here located to the north-west of the town high on a hill commanding a view of the valley. About one square mile in area, this military base extends far into a series of caves and mud bunkers with gun emplacements along the perimeter of the hill. This army base also has missiles targeted at some of the major cities of northern India. Taklakot is also a large trading centre composed of a number of distinct settlements. Off the main street is located the Nepalese market. Earlier the Nepalese traders with their families used to live on the right bank of Karnali and below the ruins of the Dzongpön's citadel, thus separating the newer section of the township from the Nepalese market. The Nepalese market is a permanent feature of Taklakot from mid-May till mid-October when the melting snow makes the passes between Nepal and Tibet passable. Nepalese traders come up from the southeast (Humla district of Nepal) via the Sher border into Tibet. The Indian traders from Dharchula also arrive here during the summer. Indian consumer goods including rice and jaggery are traded for rock-salt and wool. Talking about the Indian traders, Sherring points out: 'The Bhotias live in stone and mud huts, which are an admirable protection from the severe winds. For the roof they use cotton sheets, which admit the light and exclude the dust, and, as there is little fear of rain, they are the most suitable covering. On leaving Taklakot they remove these roofs, and the huts remain empty and deserted till the following season' (Sherring 1906: 172).

Landscape: Taklakot to Darchen

Taklakot is a bizarre combination of the ultramodern mixed with the traditional Tibetan. But its Tibetan aspect is disappearing rather fast. Most of the old style buildings are being pulled down to be replaced by Chinese-style apartments and office buildings. All-weather mud-highways (with bridges and water drainage) have been constructed all over Tibet. Late in the afternoon on the day of our arrival in Taklakot, we just loitered around the town. Beyond the Nepalese market, we saw an old Tibetan couple doing the *kora* of a one-room gompa. Three of us just followed them and then went inside behind them. On hearing 'Tashi delek' they smiled and showed us around. Unfortunately there did not seem to be too many ethnic Tibetans in Taklakot except begging children and prostitutes. All important shops, businesses, brothels, and offices are run by the Han. Police and military in Tibet almost entirely consist of Han. The most visible thing in the township is hundreds of People's Liberation Army (PLA) soldiers in baggy green uniforms.

Our tenth day of the pilgrimage was a rest day at Taklakot. In the morning, one of the guides took us to the Tibetan market which consists of about twenty-five small shops. Most of these shops are actually owned by the Chinese. These shops do not offer anything special except cheap electronic goods and clothes. Most of the pilgrims here bought plastic cans for collecting holy water from Manasarovar and Gauri Kund. During the rest of the day, pilgrims just loitered around in the market around the guest house. This market has about fifty shops selling various kinds of merchandise including fruits, vegetables, electronic goods, and alcoholic beverages, etc. There are many hair-salons as well as restaurants selling food and drinks. There are also about a dozen brothels and dancing dens in this market. In the afternoon, when we requested the 'guides' to show us ruins of the Dzongpön citadel and the famous Simbiling Gompa, we were told that these places were absolutely out of bounds for us. Tourists need a permit from the Public Security Bureau to visit these sites, and Indians are never given such permission. Once the headquarters of the Dzongpön, the five-storey Dzongpön citadel built on an 800 feet high hillside is today a series of derelict caves with half-destroyed boundary walls. Before the Chinese took over, the Dzongpön [*dzong*=fort, *pön*=lord], i.e., 'fortmaster' or 'collector of taxes,' of Taklakot used to work as a representative of the Lhasa government. His duty was to guard the road, levy taxes equal to 1/10 of the value of any merchandise which passed through his post and to decide cases of civil and criminal nature. Talking about Taklakot and the Dzongpön, Sherring wrote in 1906: 'Although there is a small village of Taklakot, yet that name is generally applied to a tract of country where there are many villages, all at various distances from the fort itself. On this ridge there is no water, and, therefore, it would be impossible for the fort to become the nucleus of any considerable number of houses. All the inhabitants of the surrounding hamlets take it in turn to supply labour for the carriage of water daily from the spring below to the crest of the ridge' (Sherring 1906: 170-171).

Bhagwan Shri Hamsa had this to say about the Dzongpön citadel:

> The route was steep and exhausted us... The main entrance to the residence seemed more like the private mansion of an Indian chief... The Zumpan [Dzongpön] wore Dokchya (boots reaching the knee) of red velvet, a brocaded Bakhu (long robe) and a tall embroidered cap on his head. In his hand he carried a rosary of beads... After a short, desultory conversation I made a request for the permit, whereupon the Zumpan immediately gave me a permit bearing his official seal for four persons... While departing, the Zumpan gave me a rupee as Dakshina (an offering to a pious sadhu) and expressed his hope that my journey might be a pleasant one... I was really very fortunate, for Tibetans are a suspicious folk. But my friend the Parma Bhutia had assured the Zumpan that I was not a spy in disguise. Obtaining the permit is usually a very complicated and difficult business, my friend the Bhutia told me (Hamsa nd: 111-114).

Across the river from the Tibetan Market, in the hills above the trail are many caves. One of these caves harbours the Gokung Gompa. Many of the caves have doors and windows and have been made into substantial dwellings. Overlooking the entire township and above the Gokung Gompa and the ruins of the Dzongpön's citadel are the impressive remains of the Simbiling Gompa. It was dynamited in the 1960s on the orders of the Gang of Four. When I visited Taklakot last time in 2004, it was being reconstructed. At the best of times, this gompa, headed by a powerful lama, had over 170 monks and was a treasure house of rare scriptures, scrolls, and

Landscape: Taklakot to Darchen

paintings. Amongst these treasures are said to have been 400 tankha paintings and four silk banners of the Shakyamuni Buddha and Maitreya which measured 60 x 30 feet. An Indian sadhu, who visited Taklakot in 1907, wrote:

> There is a large Buddhist monastery on the hill on which the Zumpan's residence stands. About three hundred lamas reside in the monastery and worship the image of Buddha kept there, with great pomp. The monastery also contains a large library. Nearby was a prison-house for Tibetan convicts, who are punished very severely, and are accorded excessively harsh treatment ... I managed to see the inside of the prison-house. A young Hunia dacoit was sentenced to death and the sentence was being carried out. He was tied up in a sack of yak-leather and roasted to death in the parching Tibetan sun. In Tibet summers and winters reach extremes of heat and cold. Among the Tibetans cutting off hands and feet is also a common form of punishment. So intense was the heat inside the prison that I was extremely thankful to leave it (Hamsa nd: 114-116).

As there is shortage of accommodation in the camps on the parikrama routes, our batch was divided into two smaller groups, A and B, consisting of seventeen and fifteen persons respectively. The schedules of the two groups were as follows:

I was included in Group A which was to be lead by the LO himself. This group was to do the kora of Kailash first. A Deputy LO was appointed to lead Group B. Chhogdup, an English-

Pilgrims stop for a while on the banks of Rakas Tal before arriving at the Chiu Gompa

speaking Tibetan guide was to accompany our group. Biru, a Nepalese, who knew both Hindi and English went with Group B. As per the schedule, both the groups are taken from Taklakot by the same bus to Chiu. Group B is dropped at Chiu and thereafter group A is carried to Darchen. Then the two groups do the *parikrama* as per schedule shown in the two tables above.

On the eleventh day, which was 15 August, we left Taklakot at 6:00 a.m. The day began with the singing of the national anthem as it was India's Independence Day. The seventy-four km road from Purang to Manasarovar passes through Toyo, where there is the chörten dedicated to General Zorawar Singh. A churtan or chörten is a kind of stupa in Tibet within which images, religious books, and other objects of veneration are buried. The Zorawar Chörten, located about six kilometres from Taklakot, is shown to the pilgrims on the return journey. After about forty kilometres we passed by Kardhamkhar. In the pre-1959 days, it used to be the seat of a dzongpön. An Indian sadhu, who spent a night here on his way to Kailash in 1907, wrote about his experience:

> At Kardamkhar we slept in the open; it was cold, and the wind blew fiercely. To counteract this we had put on thick clothes, but they were full of little insects, special products of this place. They used to bite us like fleas. Outside was fierce cold; inside there were these insects – so we were doubly harassed. However, I took off my clothes and lay down, covering myself with a Bhutia blanket; yet I shivered continuously and my teeth chattered. At this a Hunia woman brought me a dozen lambs and told me to put them by my side to ward off the intense cold.

Accordingly I slept with these lambs around me, two to the front, two at the back, two by the head and four or five at the feet, covering myself as well as my queer bed-mates with a blanket. I could then sleep for a few hours. The little animals were still close by my side when I awoke (Hamsa nd: 122-23).

After Kardhamkhar, we passed by a couple of small Tibetan settlements and ascended the Gurla-la (16,200 ft) in the Gurla Mandhata range. The scenery on the way was spectacular, huge bare rocks with snow clad peaks providing breath-taking backdrop. Just beyond this pass and about two hours out of Taklakot, we caught our first glimpse of Rakas Tal (also called Rakshas Tal) where the bad boy Ravana had undergone austerities and later disgraced himself. With its large expanse of tranquil, turquoise water, Rakas Tal bore no resemblance to its mythological images of dark and evil. From here, on a clear day, as it was when we arrived here, Kailash can be seen straight in front towards the north. Mount Kailash is far higher than the other mountains in its neighbourhood and is the only mountain to be permanently covered in snow. Its top looks like a perfect pyramid. On a clear day, the reflection of its shining white top with a blue backdrop can be seen in the waters of Rakas Tal. Manasarovar is situated only a few kilometres on the eastern side of Rakas Tal. A few kilometres before reaching the Chiu Gompa, one passes by a gold mine. The camps along the kora routes have only basic structures. No food is provided. My group was scheduled for the Kailash *parikrama* first. Most of the pilgrims want to do the kora of Kailash first and that of Manasarovar later. But Mr Bajpayi, one of the pilgrims, told me that it should be the other way round: the *parikrama* of Manasarovar should be done first as after a dip in the holy lake one becomes clean enough to pay homage to Kailashpati Lord Shiva.

The accommodation allocated by the Chinese authorities at Dharchen during 2002 was by far the worst of the entire journey. There were heaps of human excreta lying everywhere outside the mud barracks. There was no ventilation. The filthy blankets and bed-sheets gave out an unbearable stench. After a lot of cajoling and veiled threats, the manager finally agreed to give us three rooms in the new guest house. These rooms were much better, but with up to six persons

First view of Darchen

each to a small room it was quite a cramped affair. We were also given one small tent for cooking. The toilets were unusable. During my stay at Darchen, I preferred to walk about two km to relieve myself and use the creek for washing. But during my trips in 2004 and 2005, we were put up in a new hotel which has come up in place of the old dirty hovel. The new accommodation consists of double-bed rooms with attached toilets, though the toilets were not functional yet.

5 Tibet in General

Talking about social practices, Sherring pointed out in 1906 that merchants and people of position just removed caps from their heads in the presence of Dzongpön or other higher officials. But people of "the lower classes put out the tongue, not a little way, but as far as it will go" (1906: 317). He further points out that "it is an orthodox custom in Tibet for father and sons to share the same wife, the only condition laid down being that she shall not be the son's mother. As in polyandry, the eldest husband is called father, and the rest "little" fathers. This custom is analogous to the one by which a man, when he marries a widow, is allowed to marry at the same time all her daughters; for instance, a widow with daughters aged twenty, fifteen and ten would become his wife with her two elder daughters at once, and, when the youngest girl has grown up, she would also join the others in the conjugal life" (Sherring 1906: 305-306). "Each household contains for all practical purposes three or four families, and one can imagine the atmosphere in which the children are brought up with polyandry all round them, and when the time comes for a girl to enter another household, and be the bride of numerous brothers, it may truly be said that there is no modesty left in her. Merchants and officials from Lhasa can anywhere get women throughout Western Tibet to live with them temporarily for the mere asking, even of the best local families" (Sherring 1906: 190).

Further, the pre-1959 feudal system followed a very primitive and cruel system of punishment meted out to criminals. "For simple offences the hands of the culprit are tightly tied together with a woollen rope until they start bleeding, he is stripped off his clothes and is awarded 40 to 300 lashes on his buttocks and legs. For serious offences like dacoities the hands of the offender are cut off at the wrists and then dipped into boiling oil in order to prevent the wound from becoming septic" (Pranavananda 1949: 76). Talking about punishment meted out to murderers, Sherring points out that "there were many things that might happen to the prisoner, for instance, instruments might be pressed on the temples until the eye-balls protruded, when they would be removed; or the skin of a freshly-killed yak might be taken and soaked in water to make it expand, when the victim would be sown up inside and cast into the sun, the result being contraction of the leather and death by pressure within a fortnight" (Sherring 1906: 195).

Landscape: Western Tibet

Landscape: Western Tibet

Government posts were put on sale and as the period of each of such appointments was limited, the sole thought of such officials was to fill their own pockets. Such a situation resulted in complete disregard to the interests of the public (Sherring 1906: 296). The lamas of the temples owned most of the land, yaks, and sheep. They also carried on lucrative trade in wool. The villagers had to cultivate the land of the lamas as well as that of the Dzongpön without payment. Further, "all land given up or relinquished... [was]... added to the existing estates of these officials, the burden on the agriculturists thereby becoming heavier every year, as they have more and more free labour to supply" (Sherring 1906: 202). Commenting upon such a pitiable condition of the common man, some scholars have pointed out that while discussing the Tibetan situation, the underbelly of pre-1950 feudalism is often ignored (Norbu 1987).

It has been a matter of great debate as to whether the Chinese Communists 'liberated' the Tibetan people from feudalism, or imposed 'paternalistic despotism' upon them. The infrastructure has certainly raised the economic indicators, but political suppression and migration of Han Chinese into Tibet have devastated traditional Tibetan culture. Geomorphic changes in Tibet have greatly affected access to, as well as economic viability of the region. The arrival of railways and with them more Hans have further begun to put a severe strain on the Tibetan ecology and culture. As Tibet is not suitable for large settled populations, it is almost certainly rushing towards a colossal disaster.

Movement of people within Tibet is strictly regulated by the Chinese authorities. Foreigners are allowed to enter only in groups. Consequently, it is not easy to be friends with the local people and know more about their culture. However, it becomes obvious to even a casual visitor

Stone cairns and bells are the commonest sight in Tibet

Kiangs, the Tibetan wild horses now survive only in a few protected sanctuaries

Yak is the most useful animal in Tibet

that benefits of the economic development have not percolated down to the rural Tibetans and that urban centres are overwhelmingly controlled by the Han Chinese. The nomadic people of Tibet, who form a major chunk of the rural population, are coming under increasing pressure to settle down and change their mode of life. Many have already lost their livelihoods and moved into urban centres. Here they find it extremely difficult to compete with the more qualified and better connected Han Chinese. Thus, many Tibetan have been forced into beggary and prostitution. It is also a common sight in urbanized areas to see unemployed young Tibetans whiling away their time playing snooker and drinking Lhasa Beer.

The Chinese occupation, which began in October 1950 and was completed a few months later, was ratified by the treaty of 24 May 1951. This treaty was expected to initiate a much needed reform programme which was to be put through gradually and with a careful eye to the special circumstances. For a few years these hopes were not entirely belied. But then the difficult and may be utopian harmony was spoiled. The Tibetans rose up in revolt and the Dalai Lama fled to India in 1959 resulting in decades of harsh repression of the Tibetan people. "The worst years for hideous brutality and bloodshed were 1966 to 1976 when the roof of the world – and China itself for that matter – was ravaged by what came to be called, with ringing irony, the 'Cultural Revolution.' In fact, it was the 'barbarian revolution,' a savage regression into a past at its most ferociously destructive of human kind; vandalism, mindless desecration, mob-rule, violence, cruelty were the daily fruits of a blind and stupid fanaticism" (Maraini 1998: XXII). The accounts of refugees tell of many touching and heart-rending tragedies. "The forces who occasioned such tragedies would seek justification in arguments familiar from earlier colonial eras... bringing them peace, security, well-being,... roads, railways, airstrips, teaching them the use of electricity and the telephone, building hospitals, schools, factories... Such is the capricious complexity of human activity that there is a grain of truth in all this. And it is thus correct to say that the Chinese brought in (and imposed) many benefits on the Tibetans. But colonialism it still remained, of that there can be no doubt" (Maraini 1998: 366). "The Chinese improved one thing and

Following pages: Tibetan women taking out a religious procession

A Khampa business woman running a tea shop on the Kaliash circuit

A Khampa woman getting ready to sell souvenirs to pilgrims at Darchen

A Khampa woman waiting for pilgrims to sell souvenirs at Darchen

A Tibetan pilgrim

A young Tibetan yak herder

An Old woman praying at the back of a gompa at Taklakot

A Tibetan nomadic family

Tibetan couple with their child doing the kora of Manasarovar

another, but they also left a whole lot of other things in ruins. First and foremost of the country, which was poor and scrawny, had to support a population of two hundred or three hundred thousand troops and as many civilians all from China: shortages built up and prices rose. Secondly there was the exploitation of primary resources... Further depredations are to follow: mineral exploitation in the high plateaux has just begun. Chinese 'socialist and progressive' world... with its fine speeches and lovely doves of peace is in practice acting like the reviled colonial powers of the nineteenth century" (Maraini 1998: 366-67).

Tibetan youngsters

Sherring, the Commissioner of Almora, who visited Western Tibet towards the beginning of the twentieth century, was quite happy with the reception that he met in Western Tibet. Maraini, in the pre-1959 days found the Tibetans "a serene and happy nation... You met this not only in the smiling faces, in the welcome you received, practically always warm and festive, from men and women, young and old of every class; you sensed it, too, as it were physically, in the air, which constantly resounded with song- especially where there were people working. The women would sing as they pounded the clay that then dried out to provide roofs to their houses, the peasants sang as they ploughed, the nomads sang as they drove their herds of yaks, the artisans sang as they planned, wove, painted, the merchants sang, so did the mothers with their babies on their backs" (Maraini 1998: XXI). Not all, though, were as impressed by their Tibetan hosts.

Tibetan women returning from work

Tents pitched on the outskirts of Darchen

Bhagwan Shri Hamsa felt that "Credulous by nature, the Tibetans seem to be mean, cruel and unscrupulous, ignorant even of the common courtesies of human dealings. Like Bhutias, they possess no honesty of word" (Hamsa nd: 155). "The Tibetans, though stout, are not accustomed to carrying loads and do not make good coolies" (Hamsa nd: 157). Some of these biased statements do not seem to be correct of the present-day Bhotias and Tibetans. The author had dozens of opportunities of visiting Bhotia households and found them to be just like any other fellow-humans. Most of our cooks, porters and horsemen were Bhotias and all of them served us very faithfully and satisfactorily. Same is true of the Tibetans. Though not very many 'real' Tibetans are left in Tibet now, yet after getting used to their gorgeous raiment, black tents, dirt, and bad smell, we came across nomadic Tibetans, who are fellow-humans singularly like ourselves.

Mani mantra

These days the entire stay of the Indian pilgrims in Tibet lasts less than two weeks as a result of the hurried, rather perfunctory, visit offered by the Indian and Chinese Governments through the Lipu pass. The Chinese Government places commercial interests above everything else. It is impossible to rest, reflect, and meditate at the holy

Khorlo

Mani Mantra inscribed on the forehead of a dead yak

sites as the pilgrims are rushed through the various spots and are neither allowed to trek around Manasarovar nor are permitted to visit all the shrines. The Simbiling Gompa of Taklakot has been kept out of bounds for the Indians. Tirthapuri has been kept out of the circuit and many times even Khojarnath is skipped. The Liaison Officers, who are mostly stiff-necked bureaucrats of the Government of India, invariably pay more attention to the privileges than duties that go with the job of an LO. Perhaps professional trekkers and tour managers can manage the Kailash-Manasarovar pilgrimage more professionally.

Post-1981 pilgrimage to Tibet is much different from the pre-1959 pilgrimage. Before the Chinese Communists took control of Tibet, the Ngari region was infested with bandits and

Very small portion of the western Tibetan land is cultivable

freebooters. Due to the menace of these bandits, very few people from India tried to accomplish the pilgrimage to Kailash single-handedly. It was generally the sadhus who were prepared to take the risk. For instance, one sadhu, who escaped death at the hands of bandits in 1907, recalls his experience:

> Just before we commenced the uphill journey... we were surrounded by twenty to twenty-five Dakus mounted on horseback, fierce in aspect and quite capable, apparently, of murder. Indeed, there seemed every likelihood that we should suffer instantaneous death, and the thought parched my tongue and paralysed my nerves... I closed my eyes in cool and quiet meditation, with my head projected a little forward... What could have happened in those breathtaking seconds that were like ages? I know not. It was like a dream vision. I remember that I saw the chief of the Daku band standing by my side with his sword drawn over me... twenty minutes later, when I came to myself, my eyes were full of tears of love, my throat was choked with joy, and my whole frame throbbed in ecstasy! I tried to cry aloud, but my tongue clave to the roof of my mouth. Again I forgot myself in rapture. On coming to myself five minutes afterwards, I found the whole situation had changed! The man who a few minutes ago stood with his naked sword drawn over me, now knelt down before me with his head bent... Thereupon he offered us tea-tablets, sattu, flesh and his horses for our future journey. As I wished to go on the pilgrimage on foot, I refused to have the horses; tea I already had, and flesh I abhorred- so I accepted only the statu... The Dakus are a very fierce and cruel people; formerly they were like cannibals devouring human flesh; they would not be content with stripping naked the wayfarers, but revelled in manslaughter. They held that a turn round the Kailas was a full and complete absolution, for all their sins of theft, marauding and slaughter (Hamsa nd: 131-36).

All visitors to Tibet find it mysterious and full of surprises. The Tibetan weather is always uncertain. One moment you have scorching sun, and next moment it begins to hail and snow and shortly afterwards you may again see a clear blue sky and bright sun above. Talking about the weather and carnivorous horses, Sven Hedin writes:

> The daily storms were a torment. Wrapped up like Arctic explorers, we rode through clouds of whirling dust. Our skin cracked, especially around the nails, where we developed chronic sores. And at night there was a rumble and a roar, as of great trains rolling into covered railway-

A nomadic family in Western Tibet

Weaving mechanism of a nomadic family

A modern highway in Tibet

stations, or of heavy artillery rushing at full speed over cobbles... It was interesting to observe the delight with which... little ponies ate dried meat, cut in long strips. In a country where pasturage is so meagre, the nomads have to train their horses to become meat-eaters (Hedin 1925: 402).

Talking about an extreme tradition, Hedin writes:

One day we walked up to... the *dupkang* (hermit-cave)... at the foot of a mountain-wall... It had no windows, and its entrance was walled up... near the ground there was an aperture in the wall, through which food was pushed in on a piece of board. In this pitch-dark cell, a lama had been walled in for three whole years, cut off from communication with the world during all that time!... he had made the most binding and terrible of all monastic vows, namely, to let himself be immured there for the rest of his life. Another hermit had died shortly before, after spending twelve years within its walls. And before that, a monk had lived in its darkness for forty years!... Every morning, a bowl of *tsampa*, and perhaps a small pat of butter, were shoved in to him. He got water from a spring that bubbled in the interior of the cave. Every morning, the empty bowl was withdrawn and refilled... Should the immured man speak to the serving-brother, he would sacrifice all credit for his years of solitary meditation. If the serving-brother found the bowl untouched when he pulled it out, he understood that the recluse was either ill or dead. He would then push the bowl back again and walk away in dejection. If the bowl remained untouched the following day, and altogether for six days, the cave was broken open; for then it was safe to assume that the recluse had died. The dead man was then carried out, and his body destroyed by fire, like those of the saints (Hedin 1925: 444-446).

Most of the Tibetan women wear the traditional long wrap-around dresses over brightly-patterned blouses and sweaters. In sharp contrast to this, most of the men have abandoned their traditional coat-like *chuba* and adopted western-style shirts and trousers.

Religious Procession

Western Tibet does not have any regular mode of transport. Tourists have to hire their own conveyance or hitch a ride with one of the Chinese trucks (though it is illegal to do so). An American tourist had this to say about his ride in one such truck:

> Not a single minute of it could be called comfortable. With each pothole we were flung into the air to crash down with a bone-rattling thud. The Tibetans simply laughed at the worst jolts as if it were a carnival ride and settled back to brace themselves against the next series. A more subtle torment was the dust that billowed up on certain stretches, coating everything, even our teeth, with a thick grey pall... To them this was life on the road, accepted with an equanimity born of toughness and faith. Endurance is expected in Tibetan society, and complaints are rarely heard. At our roadside rest stops there was no need to assign tasks: some gathered dried yak dung for fuel while others fetched water and unloaded cooking gear, and soon kettles were heating over fires, speeded up at times by the blast of a blowtorch (Johnson and Moran 1989: 18).

Tea and *tsampa* are the twin staples of Tibetan life. Explorers are known to have deplored the unpleasant aroma of butter tea. Tibetans live on the stuff, some drinking 40 to 50 cups a day. *Tsampa* (barley which is roasted and then ground into flour) is the companion to butter tea; it is the ideal food in high-altitude, fuel-scarce Tibet as it requires no cooking. The diner pours a mound of flour into his wooden bowl, adds tea and with his right hand kneads the mixture into a doughy mass, sticky or dry according to his taste.

Tibetan Women doing the kora of a temple at Taklakot

Like all of Tibetan life, pilgrimage blends the worldly and the divine into near-equal proportions. The journey's spiritual potential does not diminish the delight of a new adventure. Pilgrimage is a time for merriment and feasting, a break from everyday routine, and a chance to satisfy the nomadic wanderlust that still seems to possess so many Tibetans. Religion is an essential part of pilgrimage, but a pilgrim's practices are often not much different from the prayers and prostrations he performs at home, although they may be more frequent and perhaps more fervent.

There are dozens of sacred formulas, each dedicated to a particular deity. The most-recited and most frequently seen is *Oṃ maṇi padme huṃ* (Hail, the Jewel in the Lotus), invoking the mercy of Tibet's compassionate protector Chenrezig. The syllables of the mantra are believed to channelize subtle energies into a potent form of sound. Most Tibetans do not give much thought to these esoteric subtleties. They simply murmur the syllables over and over, with the belief that each repetition adds to their stock of religious merit and brings them one step closer to liberation. Merit comes with each revolution of a prayer wheel (known as khor/khorlo), releasing the power of the thousands of written mantras encased within. Each parikrama of a *maṇi* wall equals a recitation of the mantra carved upon its flat rocks, just as each flutter of a prayer flag sends forth

Heads of dead yaks, goats, and sheep over bridges, entrances and other important places. Sometimes even entire dead animals are hung from roofs of gompas to keep away the evil spirits

It is not uncommon to see sex-workers and destitute beggars in present Tibet

the charms printed upon it. Prayer, parikrama, prostration, offerings – religious merit comes from all these rituals, for they are tangible links to the spiritual state, and they bring the worshipper into contact with the divine.

Much has changed since the Chinese takeover. Prior to 1959, the entire Kailash region was protected as a holy land, was teeming with vast herds of kyang and antelope, and hunting was forbidden. With the construction of highways and the arrival of the Chinese, the wildlife population has been decimated. Even Tibetans now hunt and trap animals in the area. The gompas used to be the focus of education, culture, and art in Tibetan society. At Kailash and Manasarovar, they also used to provide shelter to pilgrims. Destroyed during the Cultural Revolution, many gompas have been rebuilt but their activities and role in the society have drastically changed.

Over the past few years, the Chinese have accelerated the pace of their massive infrastructure expansion programme to develop the Ngari region. Except the odd one dozen urban centres, where Han Chinese have become dominant, Drogpas can be found on the desolate plains of Ngari. Drogpas are Tibetan nomads who herd sheep, yaks, and goats. They live in their black tents made of yak hair and do not live a sedentary life. They are "at once shy and proud, elusive and aggressive. Their baggy *chuba* were tied up at the waist, sleeves dangling down past the knees; from their sashes hung tinder pouches and needle cases of inlaid leather and bone-handled knives. Most striking were the faces: flawlessly smooth rose-brown skin, triple-plaited black braids, and eyes with a stare that might have been from another planet, so removed was it from what I knew" (Johnson and Moran 1989: 20). But the Chinese authorities are now putting into effect various policies to force them into settling down. Travel in Ngari is still not what one would call easy, but improved roads, new bridges, and telephone lines have made it physically more accessible. However, Chinese authorities still do their best to keep a tight control on tourism. They try to put as many hurdles as possible in the path of travellers. Permits are scrupulously examined at the many checkpoints, and permit requirements can change without warning. Interestingly, the Chinese have taken various measures to manage tourism, their new-found enterprise. At those sites where they allow limited number of pilgrims, they make them cough up huge amounts of money. Under such circumstances, it is certainly quite an interesting experience by getting permission from the worst enemies of religion to pay a visit to the most sacred place of four religions.

As a result of the modernization by China, Ngari is being submerged under mountains of beer bottles and plastic bags. Then there is the Chinese architecture, rapidly sweeping right across Tibet, elbowing out traditional Tibetan style and replacing it with brazenly designed buildings heavily dependent upon white lavatory tiles and bright blue tinted glass. Then there are the karaoke bars and nightclubs and, of course, no Tibetan Chinatown is complete without a string of brothels.

6 Kailash

The Indian religious tradition recognizes at least half a dozen mountains in the Himalayan and Trans-Himalayan region as the abodes of Lord Shiva. Adi-Kailash, and Mt. Kailash are the two most popular amongst them. The route which is undertaken these days by the Indian pilgrims to Mt. Kailash via the Lipu Lekh passes about 35 kilometres to the east of Adi-Kailash. The arrangements made by the Kumaon Mandal Vikas Nigam (KMVN) for pilgrims going to both Adi-Kailash and Mt. Kailash are common till Gunji. From here the route to Adi-Kailash turns towards the west and the pilgrims to Mt. Kailash continue to traverse northward towards the Lipu Lekh. Prior to 1959, pilgrims could cross into Tibet via the other passes such Mashang Dhura, Lampiya, Untadhura (Jayanti+Kungri-Bingri), Hoti, Bomlas, Damjan, Niti, Mana, Jelukhaga, and Thaga. Interestingly, a visit to Adi-Kailash is not included in the Kailash pilgrimage though it would add only four extra days to the twentysix-day journey. The best part of this route is that one is able to gain height in stages spread over a period of one week. This helps the pilgrims in getting acclimatized and it is quite uncommon to see a pilgrim suffering from high altitude sickness.

The choice of Lipu Lekh as the only border crossing appears to have been affected by the politics of pilgrimage on both sides of the border. Taklakot, the HQ of Chinese military might in Western Tibet, is the closest point both to Lipu and Tinker passes from where pilgrims from India and Nepal cross into Tibet respectively. This makes it easier for the Chinese security services to control and regulate pilgrims coming from the two countries. With the closer of other land-crossings, market-towns such as Gyanima Mandi have become derelict in the post-1959 Tibet. From the Indian point of view, the benefit in going via the Lipu Lekh is that the Chinese have built a motorable road till the border and it is easier for the pilgrims to travel from there onwards. Even more useful and perhaps the most important consideration is that by being in Taklakot, the Indian pilgrims can pay a visit to both the memorial of General Zorawar Singh and the Khojarnath Temple which otherwise would be almost impossible. Furthermore, most of northern Uttarakhand being a notified territory it is easier for the authorities to have a hassle-free control over the flow of pilgrims to both Adi-Kailash and Kailash. As almost the entire route in the notified territory

Southern face of Kailash as seen from the Barkha plains

falls along the Indo-Nepalese border, the presence of ITBP personnel in sufficient numbers along the border makes it easier for the government to regulate the entry of outsiders here. It is the responsibility of the ITBP to keep a complete record of human movement in the notified territory. Considering that the Nepalese side has been quite disturbed for sometime, it is easier for the ITBP and other security agencies to keep trouble a bay and at the same time provide assistance to the pilgrims which has been superb considering that the pilgrimage passage is rated amongst the most difficult trekking routes in the world. As pilgrims to both Adi-Kailash and Mt. Kailash use the same route and considering that the ecology of the region is extremely fragile, it would only makes sense to open as little as possible of the border territories to pilgrims and adventure tourists both of whom have been acting in the most irresponsible manner by doing untold harm to the Himalayan ecology. KMVN and ITBP with their meagre resources and misguided policies, are miles away from introducing true eco-tourism in this region. Of course, Chinese have almost completely destroyed the Tibetan flora and fauna. And now the Indian side has also begun to feel the impact. Plans are already underway to build a full-sized all-weather motorable road between Mangti and the Tibetan border. If this happens, it will certainly spell a disaster for the ecology of the region. Further, it will not only ruin the livelihoods of pony-herders and porters of the area, but much worse, true pilgrimage will lose its very essence. Of course, it will make it much easier for pot-bellied Indians to get transported all the way till the Indo-Tibetan border from where the Chinese are always happy to transport them to Kailash and Manasarovar.

Ancient literature of India locates Kailash (also called Meru and Sumeru) in Uttarakuru, a semi-mythical and semi-historical region which was situated to the north of Jambudipa (Indian subcontinent). Alakananda was said to be the chief city of this region and we are told that Kubera (also called Vessavana) was its king. It abounded with *yakshas* and *devas* and was eight thousand leagues in extent. Mt. Kailash, according to Indian tradition was at the centre of the flat world-system. According to Buddhist texts, Lord Indra (Sakka/Sakra), chief of *devas*, lived in Tavatimsa heaven which was located on top of Mt. Kailash. Gautama Buddha is also said to have visited Tavatimsa in order to preach to his mother where she was born as a *devaputra*.

Western Tibet, known to Tibetans as Ngari (called Ali by the Chinese), is possibly one of the most inaccessible and remote regions in the world. In the earliest history of Tibet, Ngari was the location of Zhang Zhung kingdom for several centuries. The Khyunglang Gompa on the Sutlej river near Tirthapuri hot springs and the ruins in the surrounding region are believed to represent the location of this kingdom. Mt Kailash was apparently a central feature of the identity of the Zhang Zhung state. Zhang Zhung was the spiritual centre of the Bönpo, followers of a belief system which predates Buddhism in Tibet. Later Ngari became the location of the Guge kingdom. The Guge kingdom originated in the ninth century. Its ruins can still be seen at Tsaparang and Thöling. The barren landscape of Ngari appears to be a most unlikely place for a major civilization to have developed. Yet the Guge kingdom prospered as an important halting point on the trade route between India and Tibet. By the tenth century, Tsaparang became a wealthy centre supporting several thousand people. The Guge kingdom, through its contacts with India, led to the revival of Buddhism in Western Tibet and became home to more than one hundred gompas. Most of these gompas are now in ruins.

Mt Kailash, closely associated with Manasarovar and Rakas Tal and located about thirty-five kilometres to their north, is a 22,028 feet high peak of distinctive appearance. Four of Asia's great rivers, viz., Tsangpo/Brahmaputra, the Indus, the Sutlej, and the Karnali have their source within a short distance of Mt Kailash. These rivers have contributed to the identification of Mt Kailash with the mythical *axis mundi* ('Navel of the Earth'), Mt Meru, the centre of the universe in traditional South Asian cosmology. Pali literature mentions Kelasa as one of the five mountain ranges in Himava standing around lake Anotatta. Mt Kailash (*kelasakuta*) is mentioned as the highest peak of Kelasa range and is of silver colour, two hundred leagues high, bent inwards 'like a crow's beak' (*Sutta-Nipata Atthakatha*.II.437f). Kelasa is often used in similes in Pali literature to describe an object that is difficult to destroy (e.g., *Jataka*.V.39), perfectly white (e.g., the horse Kanthaka, *Jataka*.VI.490, 515), or very stately (e.g., an elephant's head or a big building, *Jataka*.I.321; V.52, 53). The Buddhist text *Mahavastu* (II.97, 109; III.309, 438) mentions Kailash as the abode of the kinnaras. According to Pali Buddhist mythology, a kinnara is a little bird with a head like a man's (*Jataka*.IV.106, 254; V.456).

All Indo-Tibetan religions believe that there are three realms of existence: the sky, the earth, and the subterranean realm. Three distinct categories of beings live in these three realms of existence. Gods live in the sky above, the serpent spirits (*nagas*) below the earth, and human beings on the earth in between. In elemental terms, the sky above is the domain of space, air, and fire. The subterranean realm is the sphere of earth and water, and all the elements are present in the middle

Kailash: The Southern Face

realm, the domain of human beings. These three realms of existence seem perfectly manifested in Mt Kailash as heaven on earth.

Mt Kailash has the unique distinction of being the world's most venerated place which is the least visited. Each year only a few thousand pilgrims visit this supremely sacred site of billions of people spanning across four religions – Buddhism, Hinduism, Jainism, and Bön. The reason for this unusual fact is that Mt Kailash and the two lakes are located in a bleak and remote corner of western Tibet. No planes or trains reach anywhere near the region. Pilgrims who take the Indian route have to traverse some of the remotest and toughest regions of the Himalayas. The journey requires over four weeks of difficult and often dangerous travel. The rarefied atmosphere and continuously cold weather can be unexpectedly treacherous. To make things worse, pilgrims must carry all the supplies that they need for most of the journey. But this life-challenging experience is certainly an opportunity to view some of the almost magical scenery on the entire planet.

The *Puranas* mention seven cities on Mahameru (Mani 1975: s.v. Siva). In the north on top of Mt Kailash is located the abode of Kubera. According to a legend mentioned in the *Mahabharata*, in his earlier existence as a thief, Kubera once broke into a Shiva temple. As there was no light, he lit a candle and this attempt to illuminate the temple made him a god in the next life. Originally Kubera is depicted as residing in Sri Lanka, but *Rakshasas*, with the help of Ravana, turned him out. Brahma then erected a new temple for Kubera on Mt Kailash, from where he protects the treasures of the earth. According to the *Mahabharata*, the Pandava Bhimasena saw the golden lotus tank of Kubera on the forested hill-slope of Kailash (III.33.151). According to the *Mahabharata*, King Sagara, Baghirathi, and the wish-fulfilling cow Kamadhenu, all practised *tapas* (asceticism) on Mt Kailash. They enriched Kailash with their spiritual power and made it into a *tirtha*, a sacred place of pilgrimage.

People of Tibetan, Indian, Bhutanese, Mongolian, and Nepalese backgrounds devoutly make their journey to Kailash. Though many people come to see and walk around Mt Kailash, no one has ever climbed the mountain, the only exceptions being important mythical and semi-mythical figures belonging to legends of the religions associated with this mountain. To climb the mountain now would be considered a terrible form of sacrilege. To the Tibetan Buddhists, Kailash is associated with a Tantric meditational deity called Demchog (*Chakrasamvara*) and his consort Dorje Phagmo (*Vajra-Varahi*). These two deities are not necessarily gods as such, but are rather seen as personifications of certain wrathful or passionate aspects of human nature. Demchog is an awesome, colourful figure with unlimited amounts of energy. In the images he is shown as having four faces of different colours each having three eyes. He has blue skin, twelve arms, and twelve hands holding important objects. He wears a crown of human skulls and a tiger skin around his waist. His consort Dorje Phagmo has red skin and carries a curved knife and a skull cup. She is associated with a small peak next to Kailash called Tijung. Tibetan paintings depict her as clinging tenaciously to Demchog and inextricably interlocked with him in sexual union. Hanumana, the monkey-god of Hindus, is said to be seated at the foot of Kailash. It is also said that the Buddha once inhabited the mountain with five hundred other bodhisattvas (enlightened beings who have chosen to stay back to help others attain Nirvana). Though this is not believed by all Buddhists, what is generally accepted in modern times is the association of the mountain with the Buddhist guru, the poet Milarepa. Milarepa lived in the late eleventh and early twelfth centuries of the Common Era, and he belonged to the Karma Kagyu school of Tibetan Buddhism. Legends hold that he was involved in a powerful competition for possession of Mt Kailash with a priest of the Bönpo faith named Naro Bönchung. Another Hindu belief maintains that Kubera, the god of wealth, ruled from a remarkably rich and exotic city of pleasure called Alaka, which was situated on or near Kailash, along with eight neighbouring lesser peaks used as treasure houses for the gods. In another Hindu myth, Mt Kailash was overturned and used as a churning stick by the *devas* (gods) and *asuras* (demons) to churn the cosmic oceans in order to make *amrit*, the elixir of immortality.

According to the Pali text *Paramatthajotika*, an important battle took place here between Alavaka Yaksha and the Buddha, resulting in the conversion of the former to Buddhism. Alavaka, the king of Alavi, used to hold weekly hunts to keep his army in shape. One day when the king was returning with the dead body of an animal after having killed it, he was waylaid by the Yaksha Alavaka in whose territory the king had strayed. We are told about this Yaksha that he had a glittering palace. Ascetics often entered this palace to find out what it was. Alavaka would ask them questions regarding their faith, and those who could not answer he would drive them mad by entering their hearts. This Yaksha also enjoyed a boon to eat anybody who came within his territory. When king Alavaka entered his territory, the Yaksha seized him. However, he released

Flora around Kailash

the king on obtaining a promise from him that he would provide the latter at regular intervals with a human being and a bowl of food. The king was able to keep his promise for some time, by sending criminals to the Yaksha. Soon there were no criminals left, and each household was ordered to contribute one child to be eaten by the Yaksha. As a result of this, women, about to bring forth children, began to leave the kingdom and children became scarce. Finally, came the turn of king's own son, Alavakakumara. When the king learnt of this, he ordered the child to be taken to the Yaksha. When the Buddha saw with his Eye of Compassion as to what was going to happen, he decided to intervene. The Buddha entered the Yaksha's palace and, on finding him absent, sat on his throne. While the Buddha was there, some other Yakshas, passing through the air on their way to an assembly, being made aware of the Buddha's presence by their inability to fly over him, descended to Alavaka's palace and made obeisance to the Buddha. When Alavaka returned, his doorkeeper told him what had happened. On learning of all this, the Yaksa was greatly incensed and shouted aloud. In order to vanquish the Buddha, he stood with his left foot on Manosilatala and his right on Kelasakuta. The Yaksha's cry was so loud that it was heard throughout Jambudvipa. With all the various supernatural powers that he had, he tried to dislodge the Buddha from his seat. But he failed. Then he tried to have an intellectual wrestling with the Buddha. He lost in this too. But the Buddha had answered his questions so profoundly that he became a *sotapanna* (first stage of Enlightenment). In the meanwhile, the king's men brought the young prince and announced to the Yaksha that the child was ready to be eaten. The Yaksha was much ashamed because of the Buddha's presence. Alavaka gave the child to the Buddha, who blessed him and gave him back to the king's messengers. The conversion of Alavaka is considered as one of the principal incidents of the Buddha's life. Alavaka's name appears in the *Atanatiya Sutta*, among the Yakshas to whom followers of the Buddha should appeal for protection in times of distress. Though historically speaking Buddhism entered Tibet only in the seventh century CE, the Buddha is believed to have magically visited Kailash in the fifth century BCE. There are many impressions of the Buddha's feet in Western Tibet, four of them being on the *kora* route of Kailash.

There is another interesting legend related to Kailash whose theme is the inevitability of death. One evening Vishnu came to pay a visit to Shiva. He left behind his vehicle the Garuda (half-man, half-eagle composite) at the door. While Garuda was marvelling at the natural beauty of the place, his eyes suddenly fell on a beautiful little bird. This bird was seated on the arch of the doorway to Shiva's abode. On seeing the bird, Garuda exclaimed to himself: 'How wonderful is this creation! The creator who has made these beautiful lofty mountains has also created this pretty little bird, both being equally marvellous.' At that very moment, Yama (the god of death) riding his buffalo arrived to see Shiva. As he was entering the palace, his eyes fell on the bird in a way that meant impending death. Garuda, on seeing this, said to himself, 'Poor bird's time is up! On his way back, Yama is sure to carry the bird's soul with him.' Garuda's heart was overwhelmed by compassion and he wanted to save the poor bird's life. He picked up the bird and immediately put it thousands of miles away in a forest on the bank of a little stream. After this Garuda returned to Kailash and resumed his position at the entrance. Shortly afterwards, Yama emerged from inside. Garuda greeted Yama and asked him: 'Sir, while you were going in, you looked at the bird in a quizzical way, why?' Yama replied: 'Well, when I looked at the bird, I saw that it was going to die in a few minutes, swallowed by a python, thousands of miles away from here in a forest near a stream. I was wondering how this little creature would travel such a huge distance to meet its destiny in such a short time. Of course, it must have happened somehow.'

The most famous story is the story of Shiva and his consort Parvati. It is told in the *Brahma Purana* that Daksha was very angry with the unconventional life-style of Rudra as the latter used to smear himself with ash, wear a necklace of human bones, get intoxicated with *bhang* and *dhatura* and roam about in grave yards. As a result, Daksha did not invite his son-in-law when he performed the *Ashvamedha Yajna*. At this Rudra became totally enraged and decided to take revenge. He created two monsters called Virabhadra and Bhadrakali out of his head. These monsters destroyed the sacrificial ground as well as Daksha. Uma was ashamed of the behaviour both of her father and husband. So she killed herself by burning in fire. In the next birth, she was born as Parvati, the daughter of Himavat. After the death of Uma, Shiva became completely distraught and took up a permanent residence on top of Mt Kailash. Parvati lived a life of severe austerities and in the end won Shiva's love. Since then the two have lived by each other's side on top of Mt Kailash. Shiva as Kailashnath, playing chess with Parvati while the Rakshasa king Ravana tries to lift the mountain with his divine force, has become a reckoned subject for art; as in cave no. 19 in Elephanta and the Ellora Kailash Temple.

Another favoured subject for artists is the illustration of Shiva as Gangadharamurti, when Shiva held the goddess Ganga in his locks (*Mahabharata*.III.108,15). This legend tells us of a time when the earth was nearly destroyed by drought, and the rishis of the Himalaya begged Ganga to descend upon the earth. In literature, the fifth century poet Kalidasa created several wonderful masterpieces of Kailash-related poetry.

Mt Kailash, which is believed to have been formed some thirty million years ago when Himalayas were in their early stage of formation, is one of the most revered places in the Himalayas. The peak of Kailash, appearing like the Sphinx at Giza, dominates the rest of the ridge standing out majestically like a cone and visible from a very considerable distance. Western Tibet, home to Mt Kailash, is one of the highest, loneliest, and most desolate places on the planet. Except for a few small bands of nomadic herders the empty plains are crossed only by the wind. 'Ordinary standards would judge it a bleak, barren wasteland, but, like much of Tibet, the region seems to rise above common judgement. What is barren elsewhere becomes luminous here' (Johnson and Moran 1989: 10). Just as the landscape is unearthly, the Tibetan sky is from a fairytale, a dream. Manasarovar is Kailash's inseparable complement in every respect. The lake is female to the mountain's male, receptivity to its activity, depth to its height; and Manasarovar's depths and colours contain a mystery equally sublime. If Kailash is an immutable temple and focus for adoration, Manasarovar is a shifting fluid mirror meant for contemplation.

Lama Anagarika Govinda writes:

> There are mountains which are just mountains and there are mountains with personality. The personality of a mountain is more than merely a strange shape that makes it different from others... Personality consists in the ability to influence others, and this power is due to consistency, harmony, and one-pointedness of character. If these qualities are present in an individual in their highest perfection, then this individual is a fit leader of humanity either as a ruler, thinker or a saint, and we recognise him as a vessel of divine power. If these qualities are present in a mountain we recognise it as a vehicle of cosmic power and we call it a sacred mountain... To see the greatness of a mountain one must keep one's distance; to understand its form one must move around it; to experience its moods one must see it at sunrise and at sunset, at noon and at midnight, in sun and in rain, in snow and in storm, in summer and in winter and in all the other seasons... Mt Kailas has become a symbol of the ultimate quest for perfection and ultimate realisation, signposts that point beyond worldly existence (A. Govinda, 1966: 197-198.).

Mt Kailash is treated as sacred by the Hindus, Jainas, Buddhists, and Bönpo. The Vedic Indians refer to Mt Kailash as Meru. They believed that at its peak was the paradisiacal city of Indra, the Vedic god of storms. The path to the city of Indra was the pathway of the stars, where dead souls stood among trees blossoming with flowers, awaiting rebirth. According to the *Puranas*, the four faces of Mt Kailash are oriented to the four directions: the eastern is made of crystal, the western of ruby, the southern of lapis lazuli, and the northern of gold. It is the pillar of the world, 84,000 leagues high, centre of the world mandala, at the heart of six mountain ranges symbolizing a lotus. Atop it the sacred river Ganga falls from heaven, and after circuiting Kailash seven times divides herself into four great rivers which then flow to the four quarters of the world dividing it into four regions. The sun, moon and stars take their course about this dazzling central pivot and the multiple tiered realms of heaven, earth and underworld are spread out around it. Tibetan scriptures also speak of four rivers issuing from the world mountain: they are the Senge Khabab, the north-flowing 'River from the Mouth of a Lion' (Indus); the Dachok Khabab, the 'Horse-Mouth River' to the east (Tsangpo/Brahmaputra); the Mapchu Khabab, the south-flowing 'River from the Mouth of a Peacock' (Karnali); and the Langchen Khabab, the 'Elephant-Mouth River' to the west (Sutlej). These are the names of the four actual rivers of the Kailash region. It is one of nature's classic improbabilities that four rivers ending 2500 kilometres apart in the Bay of Bengal and the Arabian Sea should begin their differing courses in the same unlikely region of Kailash.

In Hinduism, there are three heavenly abodes: Kailash of Shiva, his divine consort Parvati, and many other deities; Brahmaloka of the creator Brahma; and Vaikuntha of Vishnu. Of these three abodes, one can only go bodily to Kailash and return after having experienced divinity in this very life. Thus, more than any other venerated site, Kailash provides an accessible and tangible link with Shiva. It is perhaps for this reason that pilgrimage to this place is so highly esteemed and aspired for. For the same reason, the heavenly abode of Shiva and Parvati is allocated a special place in the poetry and monumental art of India. Shiva, who has 1008 names, is one of the oldest gods of India. In his wrathful aspect he is the god of thunder, in his peaceful aspect he is the healer. As per Hindu legends, Shiva spends his time atop Kailash practising yogic austerities, making joyous love with Parvati, and taking *ganja, bhang,* and *dhatura*. However, Hindus do not interpret Shiva's behaviour as contradictory. They rather see in him a wise integration of the extremes of human nature and, thus, beyond limitations and specificities.

The most popular form of Shiva worship is the *linga* (phallus). In this form aniconic symbols such as hand-formed phalli and phallus-shaped objects are venerated. The *Linga Purana* describes in 12,000 verses the twenty-eight forms of Shiva as well as the *Linga* symbolism. Here Manasarovar located below Kailash is described as the yoni of Parvati, Shiva's wife; and the radiant snow-capped peak of Kailash as *Shivalinga*. *Shivalinga* symbolizes the unshakable power of universal consciousness (*purusha*) in sexual union with *yoni*, the female organ representing untamed nature (*prakriti*). The nature of *purusha* is described as being unshakable like the mountain Mahameru. *Prakriti*, in its untamed and destroying form is *Shakti*, like the floods of the Ganga, before Shiva (*purusha*) tamed her by catching her in his armed locks. The fundamental dualism between consciousness (*purusha*) and untamed nature (*prakriti*) is to be transformed into full development of one's capacity for enlightenment. This is done through the realization of reality as undivided unity and is called *Shiva-Shakti*. For a Hindu, the main purpose of making the arduous pilgrimage to Kailash and have the *darshan* (divine experience) of Shiva's abode is to attain release from the clutches of ignorance and delusion.

To the Jainas, Kailash is Astapada, the place where the first Tirthankara Rsabha attained liberation. We are told that he retired to the peak of Mt Astapada together with 10,000 monks. There he went into final liberation after having fasted for six and a half days. The gods cremated his body there. Mt Kailash became the first cremation ground of the world. Risabha's son, Bharata, considered the first *chakravartin* of India, built a temple on Ashtapada. He also attained his liberation there by fasting to death. When the second Tirthankara Ajita renounced the world, his nephew Sagara became the second *chakravartin*. On seeing the richness of the temple which Bharata had built, Jahnu, the eldest son of Sagara, was afraid that the temple might be robbed. Therefore he built a ravine around the temple and filled it with the waters of the Ganga. But, by this action, the dwelling places of the Nagas were filled with water. In revenge, the Naga king sent an army who burnt with their poisoned eyes all the 60,000 sons of Sagara. After the death ceremony king Sagara sent Bhagiratha to Ashtapada, who again directed the Ganga towards the ocean. Thus, in the Jaina tradition Kailash is a *tirtha*. It is mentioned in their hagiographies as the first liberation mountain. As in the Hindu tradition, a Jaina pilgrim prepares himself by fasting, meditation, and performing virtuous meritorious deeds. During the pilgrimage he is expected to take food only once daily, sleep on the earth, walk on foot, and remain chaste. At the holy site the pilgrims are supposed to circumambulate and make offerings. The completion of a pilgrimage to Ashtapada promises to the followers of Jainism the highest transcendental rewards (Stevenson 1999: 254).

Tibetan Buddhists call the mountain Gang Rimpoche (the 'Precious One of Glacial Snow'), and regard it as the dwelling place of Demchog (also known as Chakrasamvar) and his consort Dorje Phagmo. Together the pair symbolizes the mystic duality of compassion and wisdom which results in spiritual Enlightenment. Three hills rising near Gang Rimpoche are believed to be the abodes of the Bodhisattvas Manjusri, Vajrapani, and Avalokitesvara.

To the Bönpo, followers of the pre-Buddhist shamanistic faith of Tibet, Kailash is the 'Nine-Storeyed Swastika Mountain,' the mystic 'soul' of the entire region. They call it Tisé and believe it to be the seat of the Sky Goddess Sipaimen. The Bönpo perform its *kora* in the anti-clockwise direction. The union of sacred mountain and the lake marks a holy site for the Bönpo, the two being 'mother and father of the earth.'

At least most, if not all, religious traditions associated with Kailash-Manasarovar consider climbing Mt Kailash or sailing on Lake Manasarovar as sinful. In May 2001 the Chinese government had granted permission to Spanish climbers to climb Mt Kailash. But as a result of international protests, the idea was given up by the Spaniards. Earlier Reinhard Messner had also gained permission to climb, but he gave up the idea when on approaching the mountain he felt that he would not like to hurt the sentiments of those who considered it sacrilege to set feet on it. Of the touring season from mid-May till mid-October, July and August are a bit wet when generally Kailash stays surrounded by clouds. Moreover, 'It is common practice to go by one of the routes and return by another, and very frequently the pilgrims observe the rule, of going from left to right, as this is considered lucky and correct (*sulta*), whereas the reverse is objectionable (*ulta*)' (Sherring, 1906: 51). Every step of the sacred route encircling Kailash and Manasarovar has its own legend, every rock, hill and spring its own god: an outpouring of myth and belief which confirms by its very abundance the presence of the sacred.

The *parikrama* of Kailash, which is of 52 kilometres, begins from Darchen ('Great Flag'). In the pre-1959 period, Darchen used to be an important centre of wool trade. Now it has grown into a small shabby and stinky town. At a height of 15,150 feet, it faces the vast amphitheatre-like Barkha plain. When I visited Darchen last time in 2005, like other Tibetan towns, construction activity was going on at full throttle here. As a result, in the last few years Darchen has changed almost unrecognizably except the dirt and squalor. In fact, the most visible and audible things in Darchen are the heaps of plastic bags, barking dogs, loud Chinese disco music, revving truck engines, broken glass, bones, rags, kitchen refuse, and old tin cans. Darchen is also, sadly, a haunt for prostitutes. As it is cold and windy throughout the year and the water is generally frozen, the people here seem to wash themselves very rarely. We were put up in the hotel meant for foreigners. But the locals, especially the aggressive Khampa women, generally lurk around in the corridors of the hotel trying to sell souvenirs to the pilgrims. Darchen is the scene of much excitement: trucks come and go in an endless round of loading and unloading passengers and goods; tents are set up and regularly blow down in the fierce afternoon winds, and a constant curious procession wanders between tents, houses, and rooms.

Darchen does not hold anything of interest, except a two-storey stone building that in the pre-1959 period used to house a monk-officer (known as *Labrang*) from Bhutan's Drukpa Kagyupa sect. It had a private chapel of the *Labrang* and not a gompa. Now it is the residence for the lama and trulku of Gyangdrak Gompa. A small bazaar has now sprung up at Darchen consisting of several dozen shops and stalls run by itinerant Khampa and nomad traders and a good variety of basic supplies is available, as well as the usual religious artefacts and ethnic jewellery. A small hospital (built with Swiss help and without a doctor) and facilities of internet and telephone too have now come up here. There are also food stalls, tea shops with pool tables, and marvellous views of Gurla Mandhata to the south.

The *parikrama* route is lined with reminders of a spiritual reality, signs left by gods, Buddhas and holy men of such power that the rocks they stood upon still bear the imprints of their feet (called *shapje* by the Tibetans) and hands (called *chakje* by the Tibetans). In the Tibetan system, Kailash rises in the centre, four temples were built in the four cardinal points, four prostration sites indicate the four directions. All the mountains and larger rocks around Kailash bear the names of Buddhist divinities or divinities subjugated to Buddhism, and there are numerous supernatural imprints. Three *parikrama* paths are well-known, each of which is intended to be used by the particular kind of living beings depending upon their spiritual elevation: the outer and the longest one for ordinary human beings, the intermediate one for the *daka*s and the *dakini*s, and the third and the inner one for the five hundred *arahant*s. There are three gompas on the *kora*-circuit of Kailash: Chuku/Nyenri on the west, Driraphuk on the north, and Zuthulphuk on the eastern side.

The Labrang building of Darchen has now been rebuilt with help from foreign sponsors. In the pre-1959 period, this two-storey structure in the north of the town used to serve as a trading post and shelter for pilgrims. Now it functions as a gompa. Within the *dukhang* (assembly hall for recitation of prayers) are new and old *thangka* paintings and some statues, the main image being that of Shakyamuni Buddha. West of the gompa is the Mani Lhakhang which has a newly installed large *mani* prayer wheel. Mani Lhakhang is the site where the original flagpole of Darchen was located. When beginning their *kora* around Kailash, Tibetan pilgrims often circumambulate the Darchen Gompa and the Mani Lhakhang before setting out.

On the twelfth day of our pilgrimage, we left Darchen by bus at about 9:30 a.m. About four km from Darchen, the trail climbs up over the south-west end of the ridge to reach a stone cairn. It is bedecked with prayer flags and marks the first view of the mountain's southern or sapphire face and a *chak tsal gang*, the first of the *kora*'s four prostration points. From this point the trail bends round to the north and enters the Lha Chu valley, where the tall Darboche flagpole and the Yamadvar soon come into view. It takes about an hour by bus to reach Yamadvar. Yamadvar is known as Chörten Gangnyi to the Tibetans. The real journey begins from here, as the pilgrims pass through this chörten to receive its blessings and enter the Lha Chu valley (lit., Valley of the River of the Gods). Driraphuk is about 11 km from Yamadvar. We were to rendezvous with our porters and the yak herders near the Yamadvar. However, when we reached there, we found that they had not arrived as yet. Later, at Driraphuk I was told that they arrived about three hours later. According to the guide, this was quite usual, lost time being made up in the end by the yak herders. As I and four others had not hired any porters or yaks, immediately after arrival at Yamadvar, we left rest of the party and went our various ways, I towards the sky-burial site and thereon to the Chukku Gompa and the other four straight to Driraphuk.

Yamadvar in 2005

Yamadvar in 2002

Darboche

Darboche is located about 100 metres to the east of Yamadvar. It is marked by a tall flagpole adorned with thousands of fluttering, multi-coloured prayer flags and *kata* scarves strung out in radiating lines from the pole. Pilgrims from all over Tibet gather at this sacred place on the occasion of the major festival of Saga Dawa. This festival marks the birth, Enlightenment, and death (Nirvana) of Shakyamuni Buddha (Sakya Thukpa), and falls on the full-moon day (Buddha Purnima) of the fourth Tibetan month (either May or June). The Darboche flagpole stands some 80 feet high. On the occasion of the Buddha Purnima, the pilgrims ritually take down the flagpole and replace the old prayer flags with new ones. Then they raise it back up and circumambulate around it in a clockwise direction while conches, horns, and other instruments are played to welcome the rising flagpole. The flagpole is also carefully scrutinized by the Tibetans to look for omens. If it is directly straight up, then the year will be prosperous with healthy livestock, good crops, and no diseases. If the flagpole leans towards Kailash, it is an omen for suffering from famine, disease, and untimely death. When the flagpole tilts away from Kailash, this is also perceived as a sign of unknown tragedies waiting to unfold. The original flagpole at Darboche was said to be an exceptionally tall, 'self-manifesting' *rangjung* tree that Guru Rimpoche said was to be adorned with prayer flags. However, the present flagpole is a replacement, and despite the fact that it lacks the original's *neupa* (vital power), it is still believed to be a sacred relic.

The importance of the Darboche location is linked to the sanctity of a sky-burial site (*dürtro*) called Drachom Ngagye Dürtro, located on a ridge to the east of the flagpole site. The whole of

Darboche, Yamadvar, and the Sky-Burial

this rocky plateau including the sky-burial site is called the Kyilkhor Teng (Mandala Terrace) of the 84 *mahasiddhas*. Guru Rimpoche and the first explorer of Kailash, Götsangpa, are known to have blessed the site. The sky-burial site was once reserved for monks and lamas. The eerie site is marked by numerous small rock cairns draped with clothing, shoes, and locks of hair. Visitors are unlikely to be welcome if a sky burial is underway though otherwise the site is deserted. Here the sky burial ceremony is performed when a death occurs among the local people. The body is ritually dismembered by breaking up the bones and chopping away the flesh. Thereafter it is fed to vultures (often dogs also join in) in a last act of compassion, a final offering to living beings. The local dogs appear to have developed a taste for human flesh! These dogs are so big, wild, and aggressive that venturing alone can sometimes be risky. Packs of these dogs are known to have furiously attacked lonely strangers. Pilgrims need to be extremely careful in the vicinity of Darchen and Hor Qu.

Near the sky-burial site is a rock enclosure protecting the first of the Buddha footprints on the Kailash *kora*, created when the Buddha Chomdende ('The Victorious One') flew here in the company of 500 *arahants*. He landed at this spot first, then at three other places around the mountain, which 'nailed down' Mt Kailash just as the demon Gombo Beng (Ravana) was about to carry it away on his back to his homeland Lanka. One can continue across this small plateau and descend back down to the *kora* trail and the river, in the area known as Sershong. The valley narrows dramatically at Sershong, with majestic hills falling down to the swift-flowing Lha Chu and Mt Kailash appearing impressively above the eastern ridge. The trail passes a series of ruined

The Chukku Gompa

chörtens and a number of long *mani* (prayer) walls before arriving at a small bridge across the Lha Chu. The bridge is less than fifteen minutes' walk from Darboche and is directly below the Chukku Gompa.

Chukku (Chöku) Gompa, also called Nyenri Gompa, is a small ochre building clinging to the side of the massive mountain across the river. It was founded in the thirteenth century by Götsangpa Gombo Pel, a Kagyupa master. Perched high above the valley floor at 16,000 feet, it blends secretively into its rocky background. The zigzag path to the gompa goes up through a maze of multicoloured boulders carved with *mani* mantra. It takes about half an hour to climb from the river bank up to the gompa. All the Kailash monasteries were wrecked during the Cultural Revolution and the Chukku Gompa was the first to be rebuilt in the 1980s. It now houses a lama and about half a dozen monks. The mountain it is built into is also a gigantic natural temple, the dwelling of Gangri Lhatsen, the supernatural protector of the Kailash region. In the past he was known to manifest in the bodies of certain men 'close to his heart,' in an oracular tradition passed down from father to son. Today the oracle is silent, but Gangri Lhatsen is honoured in a special small shrine of Chukku set off from the main temple. Like all such *gönkhang* devoted to fierce deities, its doors are shut to women; laymen enter only on special occasions. Inside the *dukhang* (assembly

Avalokiteshvara inside the Chukku Gompa

Landscape: Darchen To Driraphuk

hall) of the gompa, along the left wall are small, metal chörtens on a platform, three different forms of Shakyamuni, and some statues of Tsepame, a buddha associated with some long life initiations. In a mirror hung in the *dukhang*, one can have a perfect view of Mt Kailash. Inside the *lhakhang* (hall of gods) the dim air is heavy with the scent of incense and melted butter. At the centre of the *lhakhang* sits on the main altar a single image made of marble. The squat figure is quite unlike the serene gilded buddhas usually found in Tibetan shrines; with its topknot and almond eyes, it faintly resembles the Tirthankara images of the Jainas. It seems quite out of place among the ritual Tibetan paraphernalia surrounding it. This statue is called Chukku Rimpoche after the gompa's founder and is believed to be the most important statue of the Kailash area. The presence of this strange statue seems to inspire a climate ready for miracles. There are different claims concerning the original location the statue came from, whether it came from a sacred lake near Tsethang or from a sacred lake in India. According to one story, seven white images were magically self-born from the cloudy waters of a Milk Lake in Lahaul district of Himachal Pradesh (India). One of these made

Landscape: Darchen To Driraphuk

The Western Face of Mount Kailash

its way to Kailash, where it was enthroned as the central treasure of Chukku Gompa. Another popular story tells how an old lady on a pilgrimage to Chukku chanced to enter into a hidden cave near the gompa where the statue was concealed. She wanted to take the statue to the gompa so that people could receive its blessings, but it was too heavy. Ultimately, though, the statue spoke out and announced its willingness to relocate and hopped into the woman's basket to be carried back to the gompa where it is now the main deity. There are two elephant tusks in the gompa which are said to have come flying through the air from India. In addition to these, the *gompa* also possesses a silver-inlaid conch shell which magically flew here from lake Manasarovar. According to another legend it magically flew from Bodh Gaya to Chukku. It is said to have the power to remove bad karma in the penitent pilgrim. There is also a large copper vessel there that was brought from India by the Buddhist missionary Tilopa. The vessel, the conch, and the Chukku Rimpoche statue, are said to represent the body, speech, and mind of the Buddha. There is also an image in this gompa which has white beard and a headgear. Indians believe it to be the picture of Guru Nanak. In the outer rooms of this gompa are housed the arms of General Zorawar Singh. A rock near the monastery has a *rangjung* (self-originated) image of a conch shell believed to have fallen from the sky and absorbed into a rock.

On the *kora* route, stone cairns (called *lapse* by the Tibetans) can be seen almost everywhere. The Tibetans nurture a belief that difficult passes and steep heights are the favourite haunts of gods and goddesses; and at all such places mounds of stones are raised, having a pole fixed in the centre and attached to it flutter coloured rags. Tibetans approach these mounds, chant or hum some prayer, and add a further stone or two to pile, and tie another rag to the pole. This practice is also followed by some Bhotias on the Indian side.

From Chukku bridge on there are alternative trails along the east and west banks of the river. The trail along the east bank is the regular pilgrim route but the west side of the trail offers better views of the west face of Mt Kailash. Either way it takes about three hours from Chukku to Driraphuk Gompa. The first half of the day's route is perhaps the most beautiful of the Kailash *kora*. There are steep rocks on both sides and it feels as if one were passing between gigantic fortifications, walls, and towers. On the right, in the opening of the valley, the peak of Kailash comes into view now and then. No matter from which direction one saw it, it was, as pointed out by Sven Hedin, 'equally fascinating, baffling in its mighty majesty'(1925: 472). The west or the ruby face of Kailash makes a dramatic backdrop to Damding Donkhang. Golden marmots (*piya*) regularly pop up out of their holes to peer worriedly at walkers passing by. Many of the formations along this stretch have mythical connections, a number of them related to Tibet's legendary hero Gesar of Ling. (Gesar is the name of a legendary king and also an epic concerning his fabulous exploits. The king's empire is known as Ling, lit., land, and thus, the stories, usually sung and told by professional bards, are also known as the *Stories of Ling*.) The second prostration point is also encountered on the east side of the valley, followed by the second Buddha footprint. A local *Drogpa* family generally sets up a tent near the second Buddha footprint, selling tea, noodles, biscuits, etc.

Talking about his experience about the accommodation at the Driraphuk camp, an Indian pilgrim had this to say:

> Toilet facility is a concept unheard of here. Cots were provided but these were delicately perched on stones for support. It was very cold and windy. I was shivering like a leaf. My shoes and socks got wet on the way. Our luggage was left at Darchen, so I could not change. At night seeing my condition our guide took me to his tent. There was a coal hearth and a kettle was kept on that filled with yak tea. They offered me the tea, but I could not drink it.

Though toilets are still non-existent, things have by now improved tremendously. The 'guest house' has been repaired and a couple of facilities for food and tea etc. have been put up by the Tibetans. One Western tourist has this to say about Indians doing the *parikrama* of Mt Kailash:

Marmots (known as pia to the Tibetans) can be seen in large numbers peeping out of their hideouts particularly between Chukku and Driraphuk gompas

> (M)ost of the Indians doing this (apart from some real sadhus and holy men) are older, less fit, and fatter people. At one guesthouse that we arrived to in a hailstorm at 5 p.m. (luckily the only

The Driraphuk Gompa

really bad weather during our trek), a man from Gujarat, sitting having breathing problems because of the high altitude, met us at his dormitory door. He was protesting to have to share the room with anyone, saying, 'No no' to us getting in, and later, when we forced ourselves into the room, he said 'God is great.' He truly is, you bastard, I thought . . . . Half an hour later he was our best friend, letting his friends take photos of him holding his arms around us, giving us his business card and inviting us to visit him in Gujarat (accessed 20 January 2006 online at http://www.theargonauts.com/argonauts/hannu/090100_tibet.shtml).

The south-facing Driraphuk Gompa, also spelled as Deraphuk (16,400 feet), rebuilt in 1985, looks across to the north or gold face of Kailash from the hillside north of the Lha Chu. Walkers who follow the trail on the east bank of Lha Chu have to cross the river to reach the monastery and its guest house, at the base of the hill below. West bank walkers also may have to get their feet wet since they have to cross the Belung Chu and Dunglung Chu, tributaries of the Lha Chu, before they reach the gompa. On the altar, inside the Driraphuk Gompa is the doll-like image of a famous monk named Götsangpa, the discoverer of the Kailash route. According to the records of the Kagyupa, Götsangpa lived in a cave at Kailash from 1213 to 1217 CE. Legend portrays him as a pilgrim-monk who journeyed to Manasarovar. On his return he paused at the entrance to the great Lha Chu canyon to begin the traveller's ritual of making tea but the place was so holy not a single rock could be used to support his kettle, every stone he picked up was marked with a sacred mantra. Abandoning his cookfire Götsangpa set off on the journey around the mountain, guided by a series of deities disguised in animal form. The entire length of the Lha Chu Valley he chased a female yak (*dri*): cornered in the cave of Drira she revealed her true nature

The Northern face of Kailash at different times of the day

Near the North Face

as a *Dakini* ('kodarma' in Tibetan). A *Dakini* is one of the magical legions of female spirits who are the keepers of mystic intuition. Hence the name Driraphuk (Cave of the Female Yak's Horn). The small temple of this gompa is built around a rock cave whose walls are marked with indentations made by the female yak's horns.

From the roof of the Driraphuk Gompa can be had perhaps the most superb view of the impressive north face of Mt Kailash. As viewed from here, Kailash has three bodhisattvas in the shape of mountains arrayed by its side. The first of these located to the west is Chakna Dorje or Vajrapani, the wrathful Bodhisattva of Energy whose name means 'thunderbolt in hand.' The second one located to the east is Jampelyang or Manjusri. He is the Bodhisattva of Insight, usually depicted holding a sword, which symbolizes discriminative awareness, in one hand, and a book, which symbolizes his mastery of all knowledge, in the other. The third located between the other two is Chenrezig or Avalokiteshvara, an embodiment of compassionate bodhisattvahood and the patron saint of Tibet. The Dalai Lama, called Gyalwa Rimpoche by the Tibetans, is considered to be manifestation of Avalokiteshvara. The title *dalai lama* means 'broad ocean high priest.' Many religious-minded Tibetans generally wear an amulet or 'portable shrine' around their necks, containing the image of the Dalai Lama. They call it 'gawu.' The Kangkyam Glacier descends from the north face of Mt Kailash between Chakna Dorje and Chenrezig and it takes a round trip of about three hours from Driraphuk Gompa to walk up to the glacier and back.

The thirteenth day was the hardest day of the whole pilgrimage. From Driraphuk, the Drölma pass is about seven kilometres. The path twists across a rock-strewn slope awash in fog. There was a steady drizzle, and the trek was back-breaking. Rock cairns sprout by the hundreds along the trail, raised in offering to Drölma and in mimicry of Kailash. An hour's walk takes the pilgrims to Jarok Donkhang (17,360 feet). A short distance from Jarok Donkhang is Shiva-tsal, also known as Vajrayogini Burial Ground (17,760 feet), a rocky expanse dotted with stone cairns draped with items of clothing. Pilgrims are supposed to undergo a symbolic death at this point, leaving their old life behind. To be re-born one must first die, and here the pilgrim faces Yama, the King of Death, whose judgement purifies him for the new life awarded atop the Drölma-la. Pilgrims pay obeisance by cutting off strips of clothing and locks of hair and adding them to the heap on the ground. Some even draw a few drops of their blood and drop them on to the earth. These offerings are meant to create a physical link between the spirit and this holy site, and to prepare the soul for its long journey between this life and the next. While some believe that the offerings made at Shiva-tsal earn the spiritual merit gained by dying on pilgrimage, others believe they ensure a rebirth in the land of the Buddha. Sometimes monks perform death ceremonies at the Shiva-tsal. The monk chants the holy mantras while the pilgrims pretend to be dead.

Shiva-tsal where the Tibetan pilgrims always leave something (a piece of cloth, hair, or even a few drops of blood) to symbolize leaving the world of samsara behind

My hands were frozen stiff as I had not brought any gloves with me. So I was keeping them in my pockets and this was making the trekking more difficult. Some of the pilgrims were already very tired. In any case, all those who were not riding yaks, were stopping for frequent breaks, some leaning against rocks and others sitting on the ground for a few minutes. It is a challenge to deal with the yaks and the herders. Those who take the yaks for docile and obedient creatures are often proved wrong. The yaks are capable of giving serious jolts to the pride of even the most seasoned riders. So never consider a yak to be a trained and domesticated creature if at all you have to ride one. Yaks never walk straight on the trails followed by humans. They like to eat their food while ferrying their loads. Thus, a yak never realizes that it has a faint-hearted person who is clinging to it for dear life. One witness describes the yak-riding Indians: 'Swathed in sweaters, mufflers, and goggles against the cold, they make strange sort of cowboys astride the short-legged yaks' (Johnson and Moran, 1989: 91). Here is advice from someone with firsthand experience on dealing with yaks and yakmen: "the yaks (and the equally hard headed but immensely simple yak herders) do not realize what 'customer care,' 'after sales service' and 'client relations' is all about! There is also no consumer court in the Tibetan highlands!... gift a pair of goggles/ sweets/spare cap/hat to the yak herder on the first day... (and)... pray hard. In god's own country you are likely to be heard."

Right by the trail at the end of the Shiva-tsal is a red footprint of Milarepa. From here onwards, the going becomes really tough. The air is painfully thin. Quite a few Indian pilgrims ride yaks here. One such pilgrim recalls his experience thus:

> The yak I got did not have a saddle, so with great difficulty I sat on it. There was nothing to hold on, so I started slipping from the yak. The yakman did not understand English or any other language. So I could not tell him my difficulty. Yak is a wild animal. It walks as it likes. It climbs sometimes, then gets down and so on.

A short distance from Shiva-tsal the trail reaches the sin-testing stone of Bardo Trang. A narrow passage squeezes beneath the flat stone and pilgrims are supposed to measure their sinfulness by wriggling under the stone. High above the trail is a large mirror rock; it looks red to ordinary people, white to bodhisattvas and black to sinners. A little further along, the much more convoluted passage under the Dikpa Karnak awaits those in need of a second opinion. Finally, the trail turns to the east for the final ascent to the Drölma-la and from here can be had the last glimpse of the north face of Mt Kailash. One of the streams that cross the trail not long before the pass is said to have the ability to purify the negative karma that comes from slaughtering animals. Pilgrims search the bottom of the stream bed for small black 'pills' that are held to be powerful medicine.

I felt terribly breathless and nauseous. Black shadows began to roll around my eyes. However, I kept pushing myself, stopping every few minutes to gulp some air into my lungs. But the effort seemed of little help. I felt as if my brain was fading due to lack of oxygen. Every time I stopped to rest, some Tibetans carrying heavy loads hurried past me! However, the redeeming factor was that some of my fellow Indian pilgrims were doing much worse than me. One of the pilgrims was throwing up even while riding a yak. When I thought I was close to death I heard some Tibetans shouting wildly the pass-crossing mantra, '*kiki soso, lha gyalo*' (the gods are victorious). I had made it to the top of Drölma La! After the symbolic death at the Shiva-tsal below arrival at the top of the Drölma La is perceived as the symbolic rebirth.

When Götsangpa, who was the first man to climb Drölma-la, came, he was guided up here by Drölma herself. At the great boulder which marks the path she disappeared in the form of

Drolma Pass, the highest point on the Kailash Kora

The Gauri Kund

twenty-one wolves; the rock is known as the 'Drölma Stone.' Pilgrims reverence it by circumambulating around it, bowing before it, stringing prayer flags (called *lungta* by the Tibetans) from the top. Lumps of butter, pinches of *tsampa*, Chinese paper money, coins, portraits of pilgrims, strands of hair, old clothing, human teeth, horned sheep skulls, etc. can also be seen as part of the offerings made by pilgrims. Tradition demands one both leave and take an object here; the strip of prayer flag thus obtained becomes a lucky amulet. Drölma-la, the geographic high point, is the emotional peak of the entire *kora*. Indian pilgrims perform a *havan* here. Drölma-la is a stunning spectacle, stretching 150 feet across the summit with thick garlands of colourful prayer flags dancing in the wind. At 18,500 feet, Drölma La is the highest pass on the Kailash *Kora* that represents the most challenging and rewarding point of the circuit. The crossing over this pass represents a transition from the former life to a new one with all of the previous sins forgiven by the compassionate Goddess of Mercy, Drölma. Every stone around the pass is considered to be permeated with the three qualities of the Buddha: mind, speech, and body. They also represent the

The third Buddha foot prints on the Kailash Kora

The Eastern Face of Kailash

Three Jewels: Buddha, Dharma, and Sangha. In the middle of the pass is a large, cubic rock called Phawang Mebar, upon which are a pyramid of stones to support a flagpole. The flagpole has many strands of prayer flags going to other surrounding flagpoles, and around the rock are placed all kinds of things by the passing pilgrims, like clothing, horns, animal skulls, hair and butter stuck to the rock, and other such mementos. The pass is a place for fervent prayer, mantra recitations, and readings from sacred texts by the pilgrims passing over, and is also a place to look for omens. Often, animal owners will bring their animals over the pass to protect them from slaughter and to give them long lives.

Drölma is a female meditation deity who is a manifestation of the enlightened mind of all the Buddhas. This benevolent deity is also known as Tara (who carries her devotees to the other side of spiritual realization). Thus, spiritually passing through Drölma-la marks the transition from this life to a new one, for atop the pass the pilgrim is reborn, all sins forgiven through the mercy of Drölma. Drölma is sometimes referred to as the mother of all the Buddhas, and has many aspects, but is most often seen as Green Tara or as Drölkar (White Tara). In spite of Drölma's infinite mercy the ascent to her pass remains a test of faith and determination. More than a few pilgrims have died on the approach, where blizzards can strike almost without warning and continuously rage for days. A European traveller writes:

> At 5636 meter there was an enormous amount of Tibetan prayer flags on a pole and along the stones, and we took a rest. It had been hard, but I had done it! Soon some miserable Indian pilgrims came up there too, many of them being too weak to walk and riding yaks to the top. Some were even lying down on them trying to hold on while puking on the hairy beasts... Poor guys... (Accessed 20 January 2006 online at http://www.theargonauts.com/argonauts/hannu/090100_tibet.shtml)

An Indian pilgrim recalls:

> The way was very slippery and I fell four or five times, but I did not get injured. In the Himalayas there is a plant called *Bichhu*. If we touch it, it will bite us. It is very painful and pain remains for hours. My porter was a lady. So she could not support me when I fell.

A few hundred metres down from the Drölma-la is Gauri Kund (Tukje Chenpo Tso, i.e., 'Compassion Lake' of the Tibetans). Located at a height of 18,900 feet it is the highest fresh water lake in the world. Hindu pilgrims are expected to immerse themselves in the lake's green waters, breaking the ice if necessary. Set in a 300 feet deep bowl, the green-coloured lake mostly remains frozen throughout the year. Usually the pilgrims ignore the ablutions mandated by scriptures and hurry past.

The trail down is barren, steep and rocky, through an endless boulder field. It takes about an hour from Gauri Kund to make the long 1,500 feet descent before reaching the grassy banks of the Lham Chu Khir. There are the remains of a stone hut where the trail meets the river. This place is marked by a huge rock topped by the *kora*'s third Buddha footprint. I was so exhausted by the time we reached the bottom of the mountain, I literally dropped with fatigue. I and Patil actually slept for about two hours in the cosy sunlight. Thereafter, we walked on the flat trail. The soft grass carpeting the ground is a relief to the weary feet, the liquid whisper of rivulets and streams welcome after the dry grey dust of the pass. Nomads' black tents (known as *baghur*) dot

The Guest House at Zhongzerbu with the Zutulphuk Gompa behind it

View of the Rakas Tal and Gurla Mandhata from the ridge above Darchen

the green slopes of this gentler side of the *kora*, and their yaks graze placidly by the trail. Nomads can live anywhere, it seems; fresh water and grass are all their herds need, and this gives them an enviable independence. Although the eastern valley is not as spectacular as the other side of the *kora*, it possesses its own subtle beauty. Everywhere is the sound of water, gurgling in rivulets and dripping of rocks. There are routes on both sides of the river. The east bank trail presents a better view and less marshy ground, but it requires a lot of boulder-hopping and wading back across the river at some point. A short distance ahead a valley comes down from the Khando Sanglam-la to join the main trail. This valley provides the only glimpse of Mt Kailash's eastern or crystal face. The third prostration point of the *kora* is at the mouth of this valley. From here Zhongzerbu where the Zuthulphuk (or Tsumtul-pu, i.e., 'Miracle Cave') Gompa (16,000 feet) is located about two hours' walk along the river. By this point the river changes its name to Zhong Chu '(Fortress River'). As the distance to be covered is quite long, no unnecessary pit stops should be made except for food. On the way, there was a little drizzle and both of us took shelter in a Tibetan tea shop. It was a nice little tent with warm samovars and seven or eight flasks. Many Tibetans were having tea and eatables. We also joined them and sat on the floor on a carpet. After having had six or seven cups of yak tea, we moved ahead. By the time we made it to Zhongzerbu, it was 3:00 p.m. Every body was exhausted. We cooked our dinner immediately and hit the sacks. The beds were made of wooden planks placed on stones. The quilts were extremely dirty.

The cave at Zuthulphuk is a special site, known for being the place where Milarepa and Naro Bönchung had one of their legendary contests. An interesting legend about Zuthulphuk

Gompa relates to Milarepa and the Bönpo shaman Naro Bönchung meeting at the spot where the gompa was later built, the former journeying around Kailash clockwise and the latter anti-clockwise. Finding the argument futile about whose direction was the right one to follow, Naro Bönchung lost his equanimity and hurled an enormous boulder at Milarepa who nimbly caught it. To dispel doubts in disbelievers, Milarepa left his fingerprints on the rock, by the side of which a gompa came up later on. Milarepa's meditation cave is the gompa's main shrine. The miracle that gives its name to the gompa is at the back of the main hall. Needing shelter from the rain, Milarepa and Naro Bönchung agreed to jointly construct a cave. Milarepa would build the roof, and Naro Bönchung would be responsible for the walls. Milarepa amazed Bönchung by building his roof and making it float in the air without any walls. Bönchung quit the competition, so Milarepa went ahead and finished the project by adding walls to his roof and making the cave. Thus, it was an easy victory for Buddhism. Milarepa then decided the roof was too high and went outside and pressed it down with his foot, leaving a footprint. Back inside he realized, he had pushed it down a bit too much. So he shoved it up a little. All this activity resulted in his hand and head prints on the sealing and the footprint on the roof. Inside the cave, pilgrims kneel to venerate an image of Milarepa seated in characteristic pose, right hand cupped behind his ear as if listening to an inner voice.

After the shelter building contest, the two had another final contest to decide who could be the possessor of Mt Kailash. The contest was a race to see who could reach the summit first. Naro

Kailash and Nandi Parvat

The Gyangdrak Gompa

Bönchung set off first early in the morning, flying towards the mountain upon his magical drum (*damru*). Milarepa remained in bed until the Bönpo priest was nearly at the summit, then on a ray of the rising sun arrived on top before his rival. Naro Bönchung fell down in defeat and as he was tumbling down his drum sliced a deep groove on the southern face. This cleft is known to the Hindus as the 'Stairway to Heaven.' The defeated Naro Bönchung begged permission to continue circumambulating around the mountain counterclockwise in the Bön manner. He also requested for a place to stay from where he could see the mountain. The victorious Milarepa agreed. Tossing a handful of Kailash's snow onto a nearby peak to the east, he offered it as a dwelling place to the priest. This summit is now called Bönri (the 'Bön Mountain), and on the lower flanks is the reconstructed Bönri Gompa.

Some of the most venerated objects within the gompa are some stone relics with *rangjung* footprints on them that are said to belong to Götsangpa, Karmapa, and Milarepa. There is also a trident carved out of stone called Mile Changkha from perhaps the eleventh century that is said to have belonged to Milarepa. Though part of it was damaged during the Cultural Revolution, the stone trident is considered to be a rediscovered treasure that contributes to the strength of Buddhism in the Kailash region. In the Zutulphuk cave, the most important object is an image of Milarepa made of a precious metal which was supposedly created by the sage himself before he died. Next to the gompa is the Changchub chörten, which also belonged to Milarepa. There is a round protuberance near the altar which Milarepa had declared as having the power to bless and protect. Around the Zutulphuk Gompa are vast conglomerations of *mani* stones and huge piles of rock with mantras and scriptures carved on them. There are also remains of several large stupas here. Above the gompa are a few small caves where hermits used to live. Now they are only rarely used by nomads and pilgrims but can certainly be used as shelter during an emergency. The guest house at Zutulphuk gompa is quite primitive and has only about half a dozen rooms.

Trek on the fourteenth day from Zhongzerbu to Darchen was a cake walk. We began our trek at 8:00 a.m. and arrived at Darchen in about three hours. Where the trail emerges on to the plain, there is the fourth prostration point. Along the way one can see a lot of *mani* walls embellished with yak skulls. Just before the valley rejoins the Barkha Plain, the earth explodes in a last display of colour, as if in benediction and farewell. Tibetans call this place the 'Gold and Red Cliffs,' a fairyland canyon splashed with explosions of mineral colour. Orange boulders tumbled down blue slope; a few steps later the hues are green and purple, red and black, every possible shade summoned forth from the earth in a final display of the *kora*'s wonders. Each twist of the narrow path reveals new combinations of colour, but the grand finale is to turn and look back at the whole display spread out behind.

Tirthapuri, also known as Pretapuri, located on the right bank of Sutlej river, is about 70 km to the north-west of Darchen. Tirthapuri is where Guru Rimpoche meditated and performed miracles. It is considered the third most holy pilgrimage site in west Tibet. The view of the river from Tirthapuri is splendid. The *parikrama* of Tirthapuri takes about one hour; however, it is worth taking extra time to explore the monastic caves. Tirthapuri is the legendry spot where the demon Bhasmasura lost a fight to a Hindu god and was burnt to ashes, thus, righteousness

The Selung Gompa

overcoming unrighteousness. It is said that the boiling hot water that spouts from the ground cures many skin diseases.

At a distance of about five kilometres to the north of Darchen is located the Gyangdrak or Gyandruk Gompa. Now a motorable road has been constructed and jeeps can be hired at Darchen to reach this gompa. This gompa is a branch of the Drigung Gompa (Drebung, east of Lhasa). Following a vision, this gompa was founded by the Jigten Sumgon of Drigung Kagyupa sect of Buddhism as an administrative centre for overseeing the multitudes of meditators sent to the Kailash region. Gyangdrak was the personal residence of Guya Gangpa, the first Drigungpa administrator, who was responsible for governing the estates donated to the Drigungpa by the King of Guge to support the Kailash monks. Later, when in the fifteenth century Drigung Kagyupa sect fell on bad days, most of the gompas in Western Tibet, including this gompa, were 'leased' to the Drukpa Kagyupa sect of Bhutan. These gompas were under the control of the Bhutanese till the Chinese takeover. Like all religious structures around Kailash, Gyangdrak was also destroyed during the Cultural Revolution. It is the largest of the Mt Kailash gompas and was also the first gompa to be built in the Kailash region. Monks from the Drigung Kagyupa sect began the reconstruction and restoration work in 1983. Now the three buildings that make up the complex have been fully restored. The primary structure on top of the hillock has the *dukhang* (assembly hall) within. The other two structures are the kitchen and living quarters of the monks. In the *dukhang*, the main images are statues of Guru Rimpoche, Palden Lhamo, Drigung Kyopön, and Apchi (protectress of Drigung Gompa). On chörtens near the gompa entrance, pilgrims deposit *tsa-tsa*s. The founder of the Bön tradition, Shenrab Miwoche, reportedly stayed at this site.

Other than Gyangdrak Gompa, Selung (Gray Valley), also known as Serlung, is the other gompa at Mt Kailash that does not fall on the main pilgrimage *kora*. It is about two miles west of Gyangdrak. This gompa, the smallest of the five Kailash gompas, is located on the western side of Selung Chu. A small temple is upstairs, and residence rooms for monks and nuns are on both levels. There is a trail (partly motorable) heading back directly to Darchen from Selung. Though the summit of Kailash is visible from Darchen, but the best views of the mountain can be had from near the Selung Gompa. The trail to Selung from Gyangdrak starts near the chörtens behind the monks' residences. It climbs the far west ride (16,950 feet) and then descends to the Selung Chu. Up the valley from Selung is the route to Sheldra, site of the inner pilgrimage circuit of Mt Kailash. From here there is a trail going directly to Darboche. Near the base of Kailash are the Serdung Chuksum (Nineteen Reliquary Chörtens), where relics of the former Gyangdrak administrators were enshrined. Many meditation caves are also found here. The inner *kora* follows the base of the mountain east to twin-lakes of Tso Kapala, neighbouring glacial lakes said to have black water in one and white in the other. According to tradition, only those who have done the *kora* of Kailash at least twelve times can perform the inner *kora* and visit these sacred lakes. About two kilometres downstream from Selung Gompa, the Chinese have established a plant to harvest the waters of the Selung. Strangely, one Indians sadhu who called himself Giri Maharaj claimed that he was the one who had actually persuaded the local authorities for this project so that 'devotees' could get holy water throughout the world!

7 Manasarovar

The Tibetan name for Manasarovar is *Mapham Yutso* which means the 'Unconquerable Turquoise Lake.' It is also known as *Tso Rimpoche* (Precious Lake) and is located in the basin of the Barkha plains. The name 'Manasarovar', i.e., *manas* ('mind' or 'consciousness') + *sarovar* (lake) means 'Lake of Consciousness and Enlightenment.' According to a legend as mentioned in the *Ramayana*, this lake was created by the mind of Brahma at the request of ascetics who needed a water source for their daily religious ablutions (1.23.7-8). This holiest of lakes of the world, located thirty-six kilometres southeast of Mount Kailash, is like a giant magic mirror. Situated at a height of 14,900 feet from the sea level, it is the highest fresh water lake on earth. Together with Raksas/Rakas Tal (also called *Ravana Hridaya*), Manasarovar has been venerated for at least 3,000 years. According to a Hindu legend, Rakas Tal (the Lake of Demons), located 14,850 feet above sea level, got its name from the fact that Ravana, the Raksas king of Sri Lanka, who had meditated on the banks of this lake and was awarded powers equal to Shiva's, had disgraced himself by kidnapping Sita, the wife of Rama. Many myths and an uncountable number of sages have been associated with these two lakes.

On a clear day, Mount Kailash can be seen from the shores of Manasarovar to the northwest. To the south of Manasarovar rise the five sister peaks of Gurla Mandhata. With a circumference of ninety-one kilometres and a maximum depth of 230 feet, this lake is viewed as an eight-petalled lotus or a mandala-square with four doors to the cardinal directions. A person who has the wisdom eye can see on its eastern shore *jambuvriksh*, the tree of life. Buddha blesses this lake and sits along with his 500 bodhisattvas (enlightened beings) on lotus flowers blooming in it. For the shamans, the holy water from the lake purifies the pollution of being born from a human womb. A ritual bath in the lake endows a shaman with divine wisdom enabling him to work as a mediator between the worlds of gods and humans. Thus, he can interpret *devavani* (godly speech) to his lay devotees, thereby solving their dilemmas. It is also where Shiva and Parvati bathe. Hindus do the ninety-one kilometre *parikrama* of Manasarovar made longer and more difficult by marshes and overflowing streams. Tibetans, being more pragmatic, often perform

Moon Rise on the Manasarovar

their *kora* in the winter, when the streams are frozen and the route shorter. Those pilgrims who perform the complete *parikrama* on foot take three to four days. However, nowadays most of the visitors, including Indian pilgrims, do the *parikrama* by trucks, buses or 4WD Toyota vehicles.

An historical issue which arises concerns Manasarovar which, at least in recent times, has been considered auspicious, in contrast to Rakas Tal, envisaged as inauspicious. Frits Staal has proposed that this is a comparatively recent understanding, and that the early Buddhist pilgrims who reached the region via the Sutlej identified Rakas Tal as Lake Anotatta, described in Pali scriptures as the lake where the Buddha had bathed. He argues that later Hindu pilgrims identified Manasarovar as the auspicious lake due to its location on the right-hand side of the mountain in the view of the pilgrims coming from the south. Others have suggested the possibility that initially only one lake existed.

An Englishman called Drummond, Commissioner of Bareilly, was the first person to launch a boat upon the waters of the Manasarovar in 1855. The Tibetan official in charge of this area was apparently decapitated by order of the Lhasa government for permitting such terrible sacrilege (Sherring 1906: 272-273).

There is an interesting story associated with Manasarovar. It is about the Earth and Vishnu. In this story, Vishnu was a king. Once the Earth went to him as a woman and said: 'You are the most handsome man I have ever seen. Seeing your handsomeness, I have abandoned all my husbands as they have grown old and I still remain young. I want to be your wife.' At this the king said: 'I shall be happy to marry you, but there is one condition. You shall have to become a sati when I die.' She agreed to this and the two got married. However, when the king grew old, the Earth was still young as ever. So she refused to become a sati. The king was incensed and he

Gurla Mandhata and Manasarovar

chased her everywhere. Finally, he caught her on the banks of Manasarovar. Having caught her, he chopped her head off. But, still she did not die as the Earth must always be young.

It is believed that gods come to bathe every morning in this lake between 3:00 and 5:00. This time is called '*Brahmamuhurta*.' Hindus believe that deliverance is assured for people who take dip in the holy waters of Manasarovar. Even drinking the waters of the lake frees a human being from sins committed in a hundred lives. Every Indian pilgrim, thus, must take a dip in the cold waters of the Manasarovar at least once, though taking one dip for every loved one (dead or alive) is considered the ultimate. But taking a dip in the ice-cold waters is not everyone's cup of tea. One Indian Sadhu who came here in 1907 mentions his own experience of bathing in the Manasarovar as follows:

> The morning and evening baths meant regular calls of death. With my koupin (a sanyasin's rag round the waist) on, I used to dash into the water up to the waist and dip in my head. The head or any part of the body, if exposed out of water, became, as it were, lifeless. On the shore my coolies were ready with my clothes, which I immediately put on. It was not before I had lain down for a few minutes covered over by my Bhutia blanket that I could get warm enough to sit in posture of meditation (Hamsa nd: 145).

As the sacred water of Manasarovar is valued for its purificatory and healing qualities, almost all the returning Indian pilgrims carry it in varying quantities. Some pilgrims also carry away stones and dead fish from Manasarovar. 'So great is the sanctity attaching to these waters (of Manasarovar) that fishing is forbidden, and whatever fish are cast up by the violence of the waves are considered peculiarly efficacious for the exorcism of evil spirits and the cure of all kinds of

Tibetans doing the Kora of Manasarovar

cattle disease. The fish, after being cleaned, should be carefully dried in the sun and kept until the time that a cure has to be wrought. A portion should then be cut off and allowed to burn on hot coals, and the noisome smoke and odour emitted should be conveyed into the nose of the patient by close application, when the resultant effects are wonderful, a fact which is easily credible' (Sherring 1906: 273).

During the day Manasarovar gives immeasurable pleasure to watch in its varying shades of a gem-like cobalt colour which during storms turns into a churning black sea. High elevation lends it radiance unmatched by lower lakes and its fresh waters are as clear as can be. Its disc is shaped like the sun and represents the power of consciousness, and is a symbol of good fortune and fertility. But just as consciousness is balanced by unconsciousness, Manasarovar is matched by the Rakas Tal to the west. Conch-shaped Rakas Tal (Langka Tso or Power Lake), a black lake of poison, is demon lake. It has a circumference of 123 kilometres and is shallower than Manasarovar. It is the abode of the mountain god, Gombo Beng, the great guardian of Tantrism. This god is sometimes identified with Ravana, the demon king of Lanka, who once was a serious devotee of Shiva. Rakas Tal is not important to most pilgrims, but for Buddhist Tantrics and black shamans this lake is the source of their fierce power or their power of exorcism. However, for lay people it is just a place of negative vibrations. Thus, the dark forces dwelling here being too powerful for travellers to procrastinate their journey, they are advised to cast a single glance of veneration in its

Almost all the Indian pilgrims take a dip in the icy waters of Manasarovar

Tibetan Women Taking the Holy Shower on the Banks of the Manasarovar

direction and then move ahead. On calm days its unrippled surface forms a splendid mirror for the ice-dome of Kailash. Legends hold that originally Rakas Tal was poisoned. Then a golden fish from Manasarovar, fleeing the attack of a companion, tunnelled a narrow connecting channel between the two lakes, and the inflow of Manasarovar's sacred waters redeemed Rakas. The zigzag channel linking Manasarovar to Rakas Tal is called Ganga Chu. Its water level fluctuates from season to season and from year to year. It is believed that the fluctuation in the flow of water depends on the favour of the Naga queen. It was dry for most of the last century, much to the distress of Tibetans, who interpret this as an ill omen.

Nearly all the Indian pilgrims perform a yajna on the banks of Manasarovar

Guru Rimpoche spent most of his time at the Chiu Gompa

Whatever its spiritual meaning, Rakas Tal is, in fact, an important source for rivers that originate in the Manas region. While there are eight monasteries surrounding Manasarovar, there is only one, Tsepgye, on the north-west shoreline of Rakas Tal. In the Rakas Tal there are two islands. The smaller of these two is called Lache-tso. Writing about Lache-tso towards the beginning of the twentieth century, Hedin says:

> The wild geese breed, in May, in sand and gravel, on its smooth plateau. The Lhasa Government pays three men to protect the wild geese against foxes and wolves. These men walk out over the ice, and remain on the island as long as they can safely do so. But, on one occasion, they did not have time to leave the island before a spring storm broke up the ice completely. They had to stay on the Lache-tso for eight months, subsisting on goose-eggs and grass (Hedin 1925: 470).

The shoreline of Manasarovar is dotted with shrubs here and there on the south and east. Due to low hills, the lake is accessible from almost anywhere. One can see a large number of birds

Chiu Gompa

and fowls along its edges. Flocks of ducks can be seen swimming near the shores when the waters are calm. Swami Praṇavananda identified seventy-one different types of birds in the Manasarovar region including the Brahmani duck, pigeon, rock sparrow, heron, eagle, raven, woodpecker, house sparrow, kite gull, besides the butterfly. He also reported wild yaks, wild horses (kiang), snow leopards, bears (both black and brown), lynxes, Tibetan gazelles (ghurals), Tibetan sheep, Tibetan antelopes, tailless rats (called *pica*), and foxes inhabiting this region. But now the numbers of most of these animals have dwindled except perhaps the pica. The waters of Manasarovar are also receding. Between 2002 and 2005, water receded by more than 100 metres near the Chiu Gompa. It seems that construction activity in and around Hor Qu has affected the rivers flowing into the Manasarovar.

Chiu village and Ganga Chu which connectes Manasarovar and Rakas Tal

View of Mt Kailash from Chiu Gompa

The Cherkip Gompa

The Barkha plains are dotted with juniper type prickly bushes. These bushes grow two to three feet high and are sometimes used as firewood along with sheep droppings. On the slopes of the Kailash grows a sweet scented creeper which was once used as incense. According to Swami Pranavananda, a two to three feet high plant grows on the shores of Manasarovar near Gurla and adjoining spots, known to Indian tradesmen as *lal-buti* as its leaves turn red in the month of October. Funnel-like layers of ice form at the root of this plant, which, despite the sun do not melt, though the surrounding frost evaporates. Its roots go deep down into the ground, and according to the Swami, are found effective in curing typhoid and other fevers. On the shores of the Manasarovar, the Swami claims to have found an excellent aphrodisiac known as *thuma*. According to him, *thuma* is the root of a tiny creeper thriving at a height of around 15,000 feet, and is difficult to procure. However, a simple way of acquiring it is to scour the holes of the wild rats who collect and store it in their hideouts for use in winter.

The *parikrama* of Manasarovar, though spread over three days, is performed by the Indian pilgrims by bus. Pilgrims of Group B spend their first night at the Chiu Gompa and thereafter reach Trugo Gompa on the second day via Hor Qu and Seralung Gompa. Group A comes directly from Darchen to Trugo via Barkha, Hor Qu, and Seralung. These pilgrims spend two nights at Trugo Guest House and then arrive at Chiu via Gossul Gompa. Many of the pilgrims who are physically fit would want to perform the *parikrama* on foot. But sadly the bureaucrats at the Indian Ministry of External Affairs and the Chinese (who in any case are the worst enemies of religion) have literally destroyed this beautiful institution of pilgrimage. As we have shown in the first chapter, *parikrama* is best performed by an able-bodied person without the use of animals or gadgets that ferry people like goods from place to place. The whole exercise looks particularly silly when one not only wants to do the *parikrama* on foot but also has the time for it, and yet is not allowed to do so. The least Government of India can do is to persuade the Chinese Government to give an option to the pilgrims to walk around the holy lake rather than being carted in a bus.

In the good old days, *parikrama* of the Manasarovar included a visit to each of the following eight monasteries located around it:

The town of Hor Qu and Manasarovar

1. Chiu Gompa.
2. Charyip (Cherkip) Gompa.
3. Langbo-nan (Langpona) Gompa.
4. Bonri Gompa.
5. Seralung Gompa.
6. Yerngo (Nyego) Gompa.
7. Trugo (Thugolho/Trus) Gompa.
8. Gossul Gompa.

Except a portion on the north side, the whole of the *parikrama* route is along the lakeshore. This route alternates between sandy, gravel, and marshy ground. Actually, the marshy areas are the biggest irritation. Most of the walking should be done in the morning as strong winds begin to blow in the afternoon. Then quite a few streams have also to be forded though now between Seralung and Trugo some bridges have been built by the Chinese.

In Tibetan, the word 'Chiu' stands for 'bird,' and therefore Chiu Gompa is sometimes called the Bird Monastery. It sits fabulously on top of a small craggy hill overlooking the Manasarovar. This gompa is a branch of the Driraphuk Gompa, which is located on the northern side of Kailash. The main chapel (*gönkhang*) of Chiu is on the second level and is only a small 8m x 10m room. The only notable statue here is a large stucco image of Guru Rimpoche who is believed to have spent the last seven days of his life here. There are about a dozen dormitory rooms at the Chiu Guest House (also called the Indian Guest House). Each room has an ante-

The Seralung Gompa

chamber with three to four beds in each. The rooms are carpeted and furnished with tables and chairs etc. The caretaker of the guest house, a lady from the nearby Chiu village, runs a small restaurant which sells noodles, *thukpa*, etc. Chiu village, consisting of about twenty-five mud houses, also has at least three shops selling beer and some basic food items. Though different rituals, particularly *yajna*s, are performed by Indian pilgrims at Chiu, none of them shave their heads and/or beards here or elsewhere during the pilgrimage. For the last ten years or so, most of the Indian pilgrims have been requisitioning the services of a Bengali sadhu called Swami Vikasgiri in the performance of their *yajna*s at Chiu. He has been staying in a natural cave near Manas for the last decade and a half and charges about 2,500 INR for his services. Even when the day's weather is friendly, Indian pilgrims do not show much enthusiasm towards taking a dip in the lake at Chiu. But, of course, almost everybody does so at Trugo. There are at least two hot sulphur springs (called *chuchan* in Tibet) at Chiu. One on the south of the gompa is free and has a small enclosure around it. The water flowing out is extremely hot. So if one wants to take bath here, one needs to carry a bucket etc. to cool the water a bit. A proper bathhouse, however, is located on the north of the Chiu village. The person in-charge charges twenty yuans per person as entry fee. Separate bathrooms for men and women have been constructed here. Each bathroom has half a dozen chambers with doors.

At Chiu, we met five motorcyclists from Italy who had pitched their tents on the shores of the Manasarovar. They had got their motorcycles shipped from Italy to Mumbai. From there they had travelled to Manasarovar on motorcycles via Delhi, Kathmandu, Kodari-Zhangmu, Saga, and Prayang. From Chiu they had plans to travel further westward and finally return to Italy via Xinjiang, Central Asian republics, Turkey, etc.

The fantastic view from the top of the gompa helps put the ninety-one km trek in perspective. In fact, there do not appear to be many treks of this duration where the entire route can be seen from the starting point. Beginning at Chiu Gompa, the narrow trail passes between the northern lakeshore and the low hills and cliffs. Here one can see ducks, seagulls, and geese. After trekking for about an hour, one passes by hermit caves and walls of *mani* stones. The caves, dug out by Hindu and Buddhist hermits, have been used by religious practitioners for centuries. Some of these caves have been converted into permanent homes. The ruins of Cherkip Gompa come into view after about two hours' trek from Chiu Gompa. Cherkip was the smallest of the eight gompas around the lake. Once consecrated to Guru Rimpoche, the gompa is now in ruins. The ruins are near the shore along the edge of the mouth of a dry stream.

The shortest way from Cherkip to Langbo-nan Gompa, which takes about two hours of a leisurely walk, is over the headlands. But there is also a lakeshore route by the cliffs and more

Front view of the Seralung Gompa

The Trugo Gompa, Manasarovar, and Kailash

caves. This gompa, located on the west bank of the Gyumo Chu river and at a distance of about three km, is consecrated to Sakyamuni. Nomads can be seen grazing their animals in the pastures around this gompa. In the pre-1959 period, this gompa was under the control of Hemis Gompa of Ladakh.

The Bonri Gompa, located high up a valley at the base of Bonri peak (19,500 feet), is now in ruins. Before the Cultural Revolution, ten to twelve monks were in residence here. The gompa site at 16,240 feet offers some of the grandest views of Lake Manasarovar and Rakas Tal. This gompa does not exactly fall on the *parikrama* route. In order to visit it, one has to take a detour between Langbo-nan and Seralung. In between is located lake Kurkyal-chhungo. Tibetans believe this lake to be the head of Manasarovar where gods bathe. Without circling this lake the *kora* of Manas is considered incomplete.

East of Langbo-nan the route passes through marshes. From Langbo-nan it takes about four hours of trekking to reach the township of Hor/Hor-re Qu (14,950 ft). However, from Langbo-nan one should resist the temptation of trekking along the edge of the lake. There are many streams here that flow into Manasarovar and it is almost impossible to cross them. Hor Qu, located at a distance of about forty-five kilometres from Darchen, is the administrative centre of the region. There is also a military checkpoint here. Several shops here sell beer, soda, instant noodles, and other basics. There is also a guest house at Hor Qu where the Indian pilgrims used to stay before they began to be transported in a bus. Here we were attacked by ferocious stray dogs and were lucky to escape without being hurt.

The trail from Hor Qu leaves the township towards the southwest. A bridge over Samui Chu is crossed after trekking a short distance from Hor Qu. Beyond the swamps, the trail reaches the lakeshore. Here the beach is made of black and white stones which Hindus and Buddhists consider sacred. Further on, the route passes through a narrow gap between the lake and a cliff. After this, Seralung ('Hailstorm Valley') Gompa comes into view. The Seralung Gompa was rebuilt in 1984 by the Drigung Kagyu Gompa. The original gompa was located further up the valley to the east. Before the Cultural Revolution, this gompa was home to over one hundred monks. Some of the Gompa's religious property, which was dumped into the lake during the Cultural Revolution, has now been recovered. The Seralung Gompa has images of Guru Rimpoche and Shakyamuni.

Initially, the route from Seralung to Trugo stays close to the lakeshore. But after about an hour, the hills bordering the lake recede giving way to a plain. The trail moves inland by as much as a kilometre. After another two hours or so, one crosses a bridge over the Tag Tsangpo. This area is replete with hot springs and many Buddhist and Bön sites. A short distance from Tag Tsangpo are located the ruins of Yerngo (also called Nyego) Gompa. Yerngo Gompa was a Sakyapa retreat built on the site where the Indian master Atisa was so overcome with the beauty of this area that he stayed here for several days making clay offering tablets. Such tablets often imprinted with religious figures are known as *tsha-tshas*. The gompa was once consecrated to Guru Rimpoche. On top of a hill near the site is a *chaktsal gang*, which is a prostration site, and also has a large *mani*

The Gossul Gompa

wall. South of the plain the massive flanks of the Gurla Mandhata massif rise up to a heavily glaciated summit. In Hindu tradition, Gurla Mandhata (Tibetan: Menmo Nanyi) is the dwelling place of Sarasvati, the goddess of wisdom. However, according to the Bön tradition the mountain is the home of the Queen of the Dralha, an important class of ancient warrior deities.

Trugo is located at a distance of about four kilometres from Yerngo and the entire distance from Seralung to Trugo can be covered in a leisurely walk of about seven to eight hours. The Trugo Gompa, with a guest house next to it, is located on the bank of the lake with snow covered mountains providing the backdrop. Trugo ('Bathing Head') is so named because of its importance as a place for ritual bathing. Rebuilt in 1984, Trugo is probably the most important of the eight Manasarovar gompas. Trugo is the only Gompa at Manasarovar belonging to the Gelugpa order. This place must be one of the quietest places in the world. Trugo Gompa consists of monks' quarters and meditation halls. The gompa's principal image is Dorje Chang and it has about half a dozen resident monks. Nearby there are three nomadic mud houses. The guest house consists of two parts: old and new. The new portion has about half a dozen rooms with three or four beds placed in each room. The old portion also has about half a dozen rooms. One of these rooms houses a shop run by the monks. This shop sells all sorts of goods of daily consumption including liquor and cigarettes. One of the rooms of the guest house is used as a kitchen by the pilgrims. The most visible thing at the Trugo guest house is the toilet in the corner. This squalid and unhygienic toilet located in a corner of the guest house is just a big pit covered with a wooden plank. As air is quite dry, cold and sterile, solid-pointed hillock of faeces accumulates underneath. Of course, every year parts of this hillock make their way into the lake with the gushing water when the snows melt.

Trugo is the place where the pilgrims take a dip in the holy water. Most Tibetan pilgrims, however, only splash their heads or drink the water, before they continue on the *kora*. Indian pilgrims also collect stones from here. Kailash seems to embrace the lake from this angle. The Indian pilgrims spend two nights at Trugo. The lakeshore towards the south from the gompa is marshy but towards the north it is quite clean and dry.

From Trugo to Gossul, much of the southern shore is swampy and the trail skirts the wettest areas. Thereafter the trail passes through sandy expanses. About four kilometres from Trugo the trail passes between the smaller lake Shushup Tso and Manasarovar. From here Gossul (also called Gotsuk) is located at a distance of about seven kilometres. Nearby are several caves within tall cliffs. South of the gompa, a trail leads to the highest point between Rakas Tal and Manasarovar from where can be had an outstanding view of the entire region. Gossul Gompa peculiarly sits on top of a cliff and can be reached by a foot trail from the lake. The great Kagyupa saint Götsangpa had meditated here. On the lakeshore below the gompa are many retreat caves used by pilgrims. Bönpo pilgrims visiting this gompa sometimes stay in a grotto at the bottom of the cliff. In front of the main entrance is a courtyard, and in the rear is a large chapel. The chapel has new statues of Thuje Chenpo (Thousand Armed Chenrezig). There is a secret passage from the chapel leading to an inner meditation cave (a meditation cave in Tibetan is called *drubphuk*) dedicated to Gombo Shedup. Pilgrims collect their holy water from Gossul.

The trail from Gossul to Chiu Gompa follows the edge of the lake. Tseti lake is six kilometres and the Chiu Gompa is another five kilometres from here.

8 The Return Journey

The return journey begins after the two groups complete their *parikrama* of both Mt Kailash and Manasarovar. The pilgrims of Group B are brought by bus from Darchen to Chiu. Here the pilgrims of Group A also join them. Thereafter, the whole batch is brought back to Taklakot.

The return route to Taklakot is the same as the onward route except that the returning pilgrims have a brief stop at Toyo village. Indians invariably stop here to pay homage to their compatriot General Zorawar Singh. Zorawar Singh, who was renowned for his leadership, bravery, and conquests on the battlefield, entered Tibet in 1841 from the Ladakh side and conquered most of Western Tibet. Taklakot, Tirthapuri, Mt Kailash, and Manasarovar fell within the territories conquered by him. His fighting skills and bravery impressed the Tibetans so much that they began to think that Zorawar Singh possessed superhuman and mystical powers. He came to be known as the *Senge Gelbo* or *Senge Raja* ('King of Lions'). After having established his headquarters at Taklakot, he left the area under the command of his lieutenant Basti Ram and himself went to India in connection with some personal work. Later while returning to Taklakot, he was attacked at Toyo by a large number of Tibetan and Chinese soldiers. Though outnumbered and taken by surprise, he fought furiously. According to Sherring (1906: 196-198), when the General was wounded and finally fell from his horse on 12 December 1843, the Tibetans rushed at him and pulled out his hair which was all over his body like 'eagle's feathers.' His flesh was cut up into small portions with a golden sword and every family in the district took a piece. The Tibetans suspended these pieces from the tops of their houses, the idea being that the mere presence of the flesh of a man so great must necessarily confer a brave heart for the possessor. Sherring goes on to say: 'Rumour also says that the pieces sweated fat for many a long day, a sign which the most sceptical regarded as connected with the dead chief's bravery' (Sherring 1906: 198). Zorawar Singh's wife who had been living on the shores of Manasarovar at the time of Zorawar Singh's death also died at the hands of the Tibetans.

After his death, Zorawar Singh became an important part of folklore in western Tibet and began to be revered after death just the way he was feared when alive. One of his testicles and a piece of flesh were preserved in the Simbiling Gompa of Taklakot. They were, according to Swami Pranavananda, kept under lock by the managing priest of the gompa and taken out once in four years on the occasion of the Kalacakra ceremony. One hand of the general, shy of two fingers, was preserved in the Sakya Gompa to the west of Simbiling Gompa. Above all, the Tibetans, in order to perpetuate his memory, erected a special chörten at Toyo over his bones at the spot where he had fallen. This memorial, a sort of *samadhi,* is known to the Tibetans as *Sengeba chörten* (Stupa of a Singh/Lion). The chörten is painted in red ochre and every year Tibetans pay homage to the fallen warrior's tomb by burning incense. After Zorawar was martyred, the surviving soldiers of his army tried to save their lives by crossing over into India by the Lipu Lekh. However, the winter had already set in and the biting winds forced the retreating soldiers to burn the stocks of their rifles to keep themselves from freezing to death. Majority of the soldiers perished but Basti Ram and a few soldiers managed to survive the ordeal and reached India to tell their woeful story. Zorawar's death anniversary was celebrated on 30 October 1942 in the Purang region of Tibet, according to Pranavananda, where he exhibited the General's swords, shields, and side arms collected from the Nepalese and Bhotia villagers.

On Day 20 of the pilgrimage and our last day in Tibet, we went to see the Khojarnath Gompa. The bus broke down midway. The driver gave up after having tried unsuccessfully for over two hours to re-start the engine. While we were planning to find a way out of this wilderness, an open truck approached us from the Taklakot side. Sudhir and some of the other guys struck a deal with the driver to ferry us to Khojarnath and then back to Taklakot for a payment of 300

Zorawar Singh's Memorial located near Toyo village on the outskirts of Taklakot

Return entry into Taklakot is via the Tibetan Market overlooking the bridge to Simbiling Gompa

yuans. With dust blowing everywhere on the uneven mud-road, we were being tossed in the air like pan-cakes. Sudhir 'invited' me to stand alongside himself at the back of the truck. This made it quite a memorable experience of travelling in an open rickety truck on a bumpy road!

The village of Khojarnath, also known as Khorchag/Khuchar, is located at a distance of about twenty-five kilometres to the east of Taklakot. Khojarnath Gompa belongs to the Sakya order of Tibetan Buddhism. It currently houses around fifteen monks. However, when Sherring had visited this gompa towards the beginning of the twentieth century, there were sixty monks and about a dozen nuns, all living in quarters adjoining each other (Sherring 1906: 207). This gompa consists of two main buildings and has a spacious courtyard with a high fortification wall around it. The building of the Khojarnath Gompa escaped the worst excesses of the Cultural Revolution as it was used to store grain. With the help of foreign donors, the gompa has now been repaired and renovated.

The Khojarnath Gompa was founded in 996 CE by King Khor-re of the Guge kingdom, and its construction was completed by his son. A famous self-manifested (*rangjön*), talking silver statue of Jowo Jampel (Jampeyang or Manjusri, the Bodhisattva of Wisdom) from the period of Khor-re was housed here. Later, in about the twelfth century the king of Purang added two other silver statues of Chenrezig (or Avalokitsvara, the Bodhisattva of Compassion) and Chakna Dorje (or Vajrapani, the Bodhisattva of Power) to complete the *Risum Gompo Triad*. These three standing silver figures draped in silk are not the original statues, though portions of the original statues form part of the replicas. The *rangjön* stone is original. Indians believe these three statues to be those of Sita, Rama, and Laksmana. Apart from the *Risum Gompo Triad*, the assembly hall also houses the statues of Guru Rimpoche, Rinchen Zangpo, Drölma (Green Tara), and Sakya Thukpa (Shakyamuni). The entrance to the assembly hall is flanked by statues of the Four Guardian Kings (Chökyong or Lokapalas). The adjacent building on the right, presided over by a figure of Jampa (Maitreya), is the chanting hall, with stuffed carcasses of a yak, an Indian tiger, a snow leopard, and a wolf hanging in the entrance foyer as protectors.

We returned to Taklakot at 2:00 p.m. and thereafter immigration formalities were completed. Some of the pilgrims went to the Nepalese market for food and drinks and a few others bought cheap Chinese electronic goods as souvenirs. Three of us went to the Nepalese market to have Indian food and drinks. We returned well after midnight. Patil had not still returned to the guesthouse. Sudhir found him in one of the discos. Next day, we all left for the border at 6:00 a.m. Many locals with heavy loads also joined us in the bus. They all got down on the way at Pala village. We reached the base of the border mountain at 8:00 a.m. The upward climb was begun without losing any time. With the exception of five or six pilgrims, all rode ponies. It took about two hours of a laborious trek to reach the top. My water bottle was missing from the rucksack and I felt quite dehydrated. The last two kilometres of the climb being very steep, breathing became very heavy and walking unbearably painful. Memories of the death of two professors here in 1983 made it even worse.

Returning pilgrims of the seventh batch were enveloped by a blizzard on the Tibetan side of Lipu Lekh on 11 September 1983. These pilgrims were returning to India after having successfully completed their pilgrimage to Kailash and Manasarovar. One of the female pilgrims was suffering from pneumonia and pulmonary oedema. It was decided to carry her on a stretcher from Taklakot to the border. Eight Tibetan porters were hired for this purpose. The LO, Ms Sujata Singh, let all the pilgrims go ahead and she along with Dr Yudhishthir (a professor from Delhi University), Ms Sushma Bhojan (a professor from Nagpur University), and another pilgrim R.C. Acharya, stayed with the patient. When they were about 500 metres from Lipu Lekh, the whether turned bad and the porters refused to go any further. The LO requested the two professors to go ahead, while she and Mr Acharya decided to return with the patient to Taklakot. In the meanwhile, the waiting

Khojarnath

ITBP personnel returned to their camp at Nabhidhang thinking that the remainder of the seventh batch from Taklakot were not coming. These two professors lost their way in the blizzard and perished less than 100 metres off the course from Lipu Lekh. Their bodies were discovered the next day by the ITBP and carried to Kalapani for cremation. Acharya and Singh began their nightmarish journey to Taklakot. Though suffering intensely from cold, fatigue, and hunger, the party managed to reach Taklakot alive next morning. The ITBP alerted the Ministry of External Affairs that five pilgrims were feared dead. The Ministry of External Affairs in turn contacted the Chinese Embassy, who a day later informed that three of the pilgrims had actually survived the ordeal! For the first time, an Indian helicopter was allowed into Chinese territory to bring back the stranded pilgrims. After one unsuccessful attempt, the helicopter was able to land in Taklakot and the three pilgrims were airlifted to Bareilly. The eighth batch returned from Lipu Lekh itself, thus, abandoning its plans to complete the pilgrimage.

Three Tibetan bodhisattvas in the Khojarnath Temple. Indians believe them to be the images of Lakshman, Rama, and Sita

However, our cross-over into India went without any hitch except that the carcass of a pony about a hundred feet from the top reminded one of the uncertainty that life faces in this part of the world. It was a very clear day. We were greeted by the ITBP jawans and porters with shouts of *Bharat mata ki jai* and *Om namah shivaya*. I was happy to see my porter Harak Singh again. Two of the returning porters were not hired by anybody. I hired them to pick up plastic garbage till Mangti.

Downward trekking towards Nabhidhang from the top of the pass was quite easy. In fact, the thought of being back in India made it even easier. Sudhir was happy walking at the back with the ponies. But I managed to give him the slip and joined the vanguard of the group. We arrived at Nabhidhang before 10 a.m. and had our lunch here. Om Parvat was visible quite clearly though there was not as much snow on top as had been shown in some of the pictures by KMVN. We arrived at Kalapani by 2:00 p.m. Immediately after arrival, immigration formalities were completed. In the evening, the ITBP officials organized a farewell party. The Commanding Officer gave *prasad* and medallions to all the pilgrims.

On day 22, we covered the distance from Kalapani to Gunji in about two hours. After lunch some of us went to see a temple on top of a hill to the northeast of the camp. It is a Shiva temple accessed by a steep trail. There is another temple located at the base of the same hill dedicated to Vyasa, author of the *Mahabharata*. Nearby, the ITBP also has its own temple dedicated to Kali. About 500 metres to the southeast of Gunji camp is the confluence of Kali and Kuti rivers. After lunch, five of us went to take a round of Gunji village. The village has a *panchayat ghar* (hall of the village governing body) and an enclosure with a chörten and a statue of Mahatma Gandhi. While walking around in the village, we heard sound of drums. A family was having a wedding. As we approached the Bhotia house reluctantly, the hosts gladly invited us inside. Immediately five chairs were arranged around a table and cigarettes, sweets, etc. were offered. While one of the ladies put *tilak*s on our foreheads, the men offered us *chhang* (Tibetan beer) in Chinese cups. Already a goat had been slaughtered for the festivities which were to take place after sunset. We were told that the commonest form of Bhotia wedding is the one in which the boy elopes with the girl. Marrying maternal uncle's daughter is viewed as quite desirable by the Bhotias. All the guests bring country liquor in varying quantities and it is poured into a drum. When celebrations begin at night, both men and women drink liquor and dance. We were invited to join the soiree but we declined politely. It seems that sometimes these Bhotia parties turn violent. As we were leaving Gunji in the morning, we learnt that two boys had been injured seriously in a drunken brawl that took place during the wedding celebrations.

The interiors of the KMVN huts at Kalapani, Gunji, and Budhi are covered with interesting graffiti made by the returning pilgrims. Whereas some of the graffiti and its accompanying words palpably exuded the grateful relief of pilgrims for having survived the ordeal, most of it consisted of hyperbole by pilgrims who had been to Kailash more than once. After giving away the free and pre-paid souvenirs to the ITBP jawans at Gunji, my personal luggage became quite manageable.

We spent a night each at Gunji and Budhi. On the return journey, the trekking of about twenty km from Budhi to Mangti is done by the shortest route and Gala is skipped. It rained all the time between Budhi and Mangti. Water falling down from the mountain tops made it worse. It was impossible to avoid getting the socks and clothes wet. When we arrived in Mangti at about 1:00 p.m. we were informed that trekking of another six km would have to be done as due to a landslide the road was blocked. We reached Dharchula late in the night.

On day 25, we left for Patal Bhuvaneshwar at 7:00 a.m. This cave is mentioned in the *Skanda Purana*. The big natural cave is quite damp and has an extremely narrow, slippery, and cumbersome entrance. There are natural idols of Gauri, Shiva, Ganesh, and other gods and goddesses engraved on the walls. Shankaracharya had installed a *linga* here and appointed a man from Kashi for daily *puja* in those days. Even now the *puja* is performed by a priest from the same family. An interesting story relating to Ganesh is depicted inside this cave. When Shiva was away, Parvati gave birth to Ganesh. Once while she was having a bath, she asked Ganesh to guard the door. While Ganesh was guarding the door, suddenly Shiva appeared at the door and wanted to see his wife immediately. Ganesh refused to let me go in as his mother was having a bath. But Shiva became infuriated him and he cut off the boy's head. When later Shiva came to know that Ganesh was his own son, he was quite repentant. Parvati too was very depressed. Brahma came to their help at this juncture and advised that if the head of the first animal sighted is brought and

Jageshwar: the Mritunjaya Temple

placed on Ganesha's torso, he will survive. Lord Vishnu set off in search of an animal and found an elephant near the base of Mt Kailash. He cut off the elephant's head and brought it to place it on the body of Ganesh. The anointing of Ganesha's torso was done with the holy water of eight-petalled lotus while Vishnu was out seeking an animal's head. Water flowing from a stone projection representing the eight-petalled lotus and below a stone representing the torso of Ganesh inside the cave are reminiscences of how the body of Ganesh was preserved till the elephant's head arrived.

A Panel at the Mritunjaya Temple

The Archaeolgoical Survey of India Musuem at Jageshwar

It was very dark and slippery inside and the oxygen was quite low. But it was a great experience. The Hindus believe that one visit to this cave is the equivalent of the *Char Dham Yatra*. In the nearby village, an ancient statue of the Buddha is worshipped. As my toe-nails had come off, I had decided to wear bathroom slippers from Dharchula onwards. While walking around in rain at Patal Bhuvaneshwar, I was bitten by a couple of leeches on the right foot. It took quite a while for the bleeding to stop. After lunch here, we left for Mirthi where we arrived at about 4:00 p.m.

We were given a farewell reception here by the ITBP. They also gave each of us a copy of the group photo. One of the buses broke down on the way and it was 11:00 p.m. when we reached Jageshwar. Here, the pilgrims paid a thanksgiving visit to the temple of Mrityunjaya on the morning of day 26. Home to one of the twelve *jyotirlingas* of Shiva, Jageshwar lies in a beautiful narrow valley hedged by lush green deodars. The main temple complex at Jageshwar consists of about 200 large and small shrines some of which were constructed as early as the eighth century CE. Of these shrines, three are dedicated to Jageshwar, Mrityunjaya, and Pushtidevi. Jageshwar temple has sculpted *dvarapalas* (door guardians) standing guard at its entrance. Although the presiding deity at Jageshwar is Shiva, the carvings show strong influence of Buddhism. Many beautiful stone images of Shiva and other deities can be seen within the temple. The *Ekamukhalinga* (a Shivalinga with the face of Shiva etched on it) is one of the rarest specimens to be found in northern India. The Jageshwar temple is protected by the Archaeological Survey of India whose small museum has an impressive collection of images of different deities in its two galleries. The collection in the first gallery consists of masterpieces that include the image of Uma-Maheshwar having flying celestials and fully ornamented Goddess Parvati siting on the lap of Lord Shiva. Another beautiful sculpture is that of Surya holding lotus in both hands and Arun, the charioteer as well as seven horses. Still another sculpture is that of *Navgrahas* (Surya, Soma, Mangala, Budha, Brihaspati, Shukra, Shani, Rahu, and Ketu). The second gallery houses of unique specimens of Uttarakhand art consisting of the Vishapaharanamurti (Shiva drinking poison), four-armed Chamunda with skeletal body and holding munda in her left hand.

After a visit to the museum and the Mrityunjaya Temple, we set out for Delhi. On the way we stopped for a while at the Kainchi Dham Temple. Kainchi Dham is a modern pilgrim centre. This place has achieved recognition owing to the *ashram* of the famous Neem Karoli Bawa. We also took a short break on the banks of Ganga. Some of the pilgrims collected holy water from here. Mr Patil suddenly realized that he needed more holy water than he was carrying. So he too replenished his stocks here. We arrived in Delhi shortly before sunset.

Bibliography

The *Aṅguttara Nikāya*, ed. R. Morris & E. Hardy, 5 vols. London: PTS, 1885-1900. The translated references are from *The Book of the Gradual Sayings*, tr. F.L. Woodward: Vols. I, II & V; E.M. Hare: Vols. III & IV, London: PTS, 1955-1970.

The *Aṅguttara Nikāya Aṭṭhakathā*, eds. H. Walleser & H. Kopp, *Manorathapūraṇī: Buddhaghosa's Commentary on the Aṅguttara Nikāya,* 5 vols, London: PTS, 1924-1956.

Bedi, R.K. & Subramanian Swamy. 1984. *Kailas & Manasarovar After 22 Years in Shiva's Domain,* New Delhi: Allied Publishers Private Limited.

Berg, E. 1994. "Journeys to the Holy Center: The Study of Pilgrimage in Recent Himalayan Research," in the *European Bulletin of Himalayan Research*, No. 6.

Bharati, S.A. 1963. "Pilgrimage in the Indian Tradition," *History of Religions*, Vol. 3, No. 1: 135-167.

Bhardwaj, S.M. 1973. *Hindu Places of Pilgrimage: A Study in Cultural Geography*, Berkeley: University of California Press.

Blondeau, A.M. & E. Steinkellner (eds). 1996. *Reflections of the Mountain: Essays on the History and Social Meaning of the Mountain Cult in Tibet and the Himalaya*, Wien: Osterreichische Akademie der Wissenschaften.

Bower, H. 1894. *Diary of a Journey across Tibet*, reprint, Kathmandu: Ratna Pustak Bhandar, 1976.

Buffetrille, K. 1998. "Reflections on Pilgrimages to Sacred Mountains, Lakes and Caves," in Alex McKay (ed), *Pilgrimage in Tibet*, Richmond Surrey: Curzon Press: 18-34.

Bysack, G.D. 1890. "Notes on a Buddhist Monastery at Bhot Bhagan in Howrah," *Journal of the Royal Asiatic Society of Bengal*, 59, 1890: 99 (64-99).

The *Buddhavaṃsa Aṭṭhakathā*, ed I.B. Horner, *the Madhuratthavilāsinī,* Buddhadatta Thera's commentary on the *Buddhavaṃsa*, London: PTS, 1946 (mentioned as BuA in the notes). Tr. I.B. Horner, *the Clarifier of Sweet Meaning* (*Madhuratthavilāsinī*), translation of the Pāli Commentaries No. 1, London: PTS, SBB, XXXIII, 1978.

Cammann S. 1951. *Trade Through the Himalayas: The Early British Attempts to Open Tibet,* Princeton: Princeton University Press.

Chan, V. 1994. *Tibet Handbook: A Pilgrimage Guide*, Chico, California: Moon.

Coehlo, Paulo. 1995. *The Pilgrimage*, reprint, San Francisco: Harper.

The Dhammapadaṭṭhakathā, ed. H.C. Norman, *The Commentary on the Dhammapada*, 4 vols, London: PTS, 1906. Tr. E.W. Burlingame, *Buddhist Legends*, 3 vols, Harvard Oriental Series, Cambridge, Mass: Harvard University Press, 1921.

The *Dīgha Nikāya*, ed. T.W.Rhys Davids & J.E. Carpenter, 3 Vols. London: PTS, 1890-1911. Tr. T.W. & C.A.F. Rhys Davids; *The Dialogues of the Buddha*; 3 vols. 1899, 1910 & 1957 respectively (reprints), London: PTS. Also translated by M. Walshe, *Thus Have I Heard: The Long Discourses of the Buddha*, London: Wisdom Publications, 1987.

The *Dīgha Nikāya Aṭṭhakathā*, eds. T.W. Rhys Davids, J.E. Carpentier & W. Stede, *Sumaṅgalavilāsinī*, Buddhaghosa's commentary on the *Dīgha Nikāya*, 3 vols, London: PTS, 1886-1932.

Dowman, K. 1988. *The Power-places of Central Tibet: the Pilgrim's Guide*, London: Routeledge and Kegan Paul.

Dubey, D.P. (ed). 1995. *Pilgrimage Studies: Sacred Places Sacred Traditions*, Allahabad: The Society of Pilgrimage Studies.

Duncan, J. 1801. "An Account of Two Fakeers with their Portraits," in *Oriental Memoirs*, London, 1801: 37-52.

Eck, D.L. "India's Tirthas: 'Crossings' in Sacred geography," *History of Religions*, 20.4, 1981.

Erickson, Barbara. 1997. *TIBET: Abode of the Gods, Pearl of the Motherland*, Pacific View PR.

Foreman, H. 1936. *Through Forbidden Tibet*, London: Anchor Press.

Francke, A.H. 1914. *Antiquities of Indian Tibet, Part 1, Personal Narrative*, Calcutta: Superintendent of Government Printing.

Francke, A.H. 1926. *Antiquities of Indian Tibet, Part 2, The Chronicles of Ladakh and Minor Chronicles*, reprint, Delhi: S. Chand & Co., 1972.

Frawley, D. 1995. *Hinduism: The Eternal Tradition*, Voice of India.

French, Patrick. 2003. *Tibet: A Personal History of a Lost Land*, New York: Knopf.

Ganhar, J.N. 1973. *Jammu Shrines and Pilgrimages*, New Delhi.

Gill, Gagan. 2008. *Awaak Kailash-Manasarovar: Ek Antrayatra* (in Hindi), New Delhi: Vani Prakashan.

Goldstein, Melvyn C. 1989. *A History of Modern Tibet, 1913-1950: Demise of the Lamaist State*, reprint, Berkeley: University of California Press.

Goldstein, Melvyn C. & C.M. Breall. 1990. *Nomads of Western Tibet: the Survival of a Way of Life*, Hong Kong: Odyssey.

Goldstein, Melvyn C. 1997. *The Snow Lion and the Dragon: China, Tibet and the Dalai Lama*, Berkeley: University of California Press.

Govinda, A. 1966. *The Way of the White Clouds: A Buddhist Pilgrim in Tibet*, London: Rider & Co.

Gyatso, Palden. 1997. *Fire Under the Snow*, tr. Tsering Shakya, London: the Harvill Press.

Hamsa, Bhagwan Shri. nd. *The Holy Mountain: Being the Story of a Pilgrimage to Lake Manas and of Initiation on Mount Kailash in Tibet*, London: Faber and Faber.

Harrer, H. 1954. *Seven Years in Tibet*, New York: E.P. Dutton.

Harrer, H. 1984. *Return to Tibet*, London: Wiedenfeld & Nicolson.

Hedin, S. 1910-13. *Trans-Himalaya: Discoveries and Adventures in Tibet*, 3 vols, London: Macmillan & Co.

Hedin, S. 1925. *My Life as an Explorer*, reprint, New York: Kodansha International, 1996.

Heesterman, J. 1981. "Householder and Wandered," in T.N. Madan (ed), *Way of Life: King, Householder, Renouncer, Studies in Honour of Louis Dumont*, New Delhi: Vikas.

Hoon, Vineeta. 1996. *Living on the Move: Bhotiyas of the Kumaon Himalaya (Livelihood and Environment)*, New Delhi: Sage Publications.

Hopkins, E.W. 1968. *Epic Mythology*, reprint, Delhi: Indological Book House.

Hopper, Sarah. 2002. *To Be a Pilgrim,* Phoenix Mill, England: Sutton Publishing Limited.

Huber, T. 1990. "Where exactly are Cāritra, Devikoṭa and Himavat? A sacred geography controversy and the development of Tantric Buddhist pilgrimage sites in Tibet," *Kailash: A Journal of Himalayan Studies*, vol. XVI, nos. 3-4, 1990.

Kelly, Thomas, Carroll Dunham and Ian Baker. 1993. *Tibet: Reflections from the Wheel of Life*; New York: Abbeville Press.

The *Jātaka*, ed. V. Fausböll , *The Jātaka*, 6 vols, London: Luzac & Co, 1877-1897; D. Anderson, *Index to the Jātaka and Its Commentary*, , vol. 7, London: Luzac & Co, 1897. Tr. R. Chalmers, vol. I; W.H.D. Rouse, vol. II and IV; H.T. Francis & R.A. Neil vol. III; H.T. Francis, vol. V; E.W. Cowell & W.H.D. Rouse, vol. VI; *The Jātaka or the Stories of the Buddha's Former Births*, Cambridge: Cambridge University Press, 1895-1907.

Jha, M. (ed). 1985. *Dimensions of Pilgrimage: An Anthropological Perspective*, New Delhi: Inter-India Publications.

Jha, M. (ed). 1995. *Pilgrimage: Concepts, Themes, Issues and Methodology*, New Delhi: Inter-India Publications.

Johnson, R. & K. Moran. 1989. *Tibet's Sacred Mountain of Tibet: The Extraordinary Pilgrimage to Mount Kailas*, Rochester: Park Street Press.

The *Kathāvatthu*, ed. A.C. Taylor, 2 vols, London: PTS, 1894-95. Tr. Shwe Zan Aung and C.A.F. Rhys Davids, *Points of Controversy or Subjects of Discourse, being a Translation of the Kathāvatthu from the Abhidhammapiṭaka*, London: PTS, 1915.

Kawaguchi, E. 1909. *Three Years in Tibet*, reprint, Kathmandu: Ratna Pustak Bhandar, 1979 (originally published, 1909).

The Khuddaka-Pāṭha Aṭṭhakathā, ed. H. Smith, the *Paramatthajotikā I* , London: PTS, 1915. Tr. with its commentary, Bhikkhu Ñāṇamoli, *Minor Readings and Illustrator*, London: PTS, 1960.

Lemaire, T. 1970. *Filosofie van het landscap*, Baarn: Ambo.

Li An-che, 1948. "Our Pilgrimage to a Tibetan Sacred Mountain," *Asian Horizon*, vol. 2, summer, 1948.

Loseries-Leick, Andrea. 1998. "On the Sacredness of Mountain Kailasa in the Indian and Tibetan Sources," Alex McKay (ed). 1998. *Pilgrimage in Tibet*, Richmond Surrey: Curzon Press: 143-164.

Mabbett, I.W. 1983. "The Symbolism of Mount Meru," *History of Religions*, 23.1: 64-83.

MacDonald, A.W. (ed). 1997. *Mandala and Landcape*, New Delhi: D.K. Printworld.

Madan T.N. (ed). 1981. *Way of Life: King, Householder, Renouncer, Studies in Honour of Louis Dumont*, New Delhi: Vikas.

The Majjhima Nikāya Aṭṭhakathā, eds. J.H. Woods, D. Kosambi, and I.B. Horner, *Papañcasādanī: Majjhimanikāyaṭṭhakathā of Buddhaghosācariya*, 5 vols, London: PTS, 1922-38.

Mani, V. 1975. *Puranic Encyclopedia: A Comprehensive Dictionary with special reference to the Epic and Puranic Literature*, Delhi.

Maraini, Fosco. 1998. *Secret Tibet*, London: The Harvill Press.

McKay, Alex (ed). 1998. *Pilgrimage in Tibet*, Richmond Surrey: Curzon Press.

The *Milindapañha*, ed. Swami Dwārikādāsaśāstrī, *Milindapañhapāli*, (Devanagari), Varanasi: Bauddhabharati, 1979. References are from ed. V. Trenckner, *Milindapañha*, London: Williams and Norgate: 1880 (mentioned as Mil in the notes). Tr T.W. Rhys Davids, *The Questions of King Milinda*, SBE, Vols. 35 & 36, reprint, Delhi: Motilal Banarsidass, 1982 (first published by Oxford University Press, 1890).

Morinis, E.A. 1984. *Pilgrimage in the Hindu Tradition*, Delhi: Oxford University Press.

Norbu, Dawa. 1987. *Red Star Over Tibet*, New Delhi: Sterling: Publishers.

Oberdiek, U. 1995. "Functions of Hindu Pilgrimage: Secular Traits in Tirthayatra," in Dubey D.P. (ed). *Pilgrimage Studies: Sacred Places Sacred Traditions*, Allahabad: The Society of Pilgrimage Studies.

Pranavananda, Swami. 1949. *Kailās-Mānasarovar*, Calcutta: S.P. League Ltd.

Rangachar, N. 1931. *Diary of a Pilgrimage to Lake Manasarowar and Mount Kailas with H.H. the Maharaja of Mysore in 1931*, Mysore: Government Branch Press, 1931.

Rawat, I.S. 1973. *Indian Explorers of the 19th Century: Account of Explorations in the Himalayas, Tibet, Mongolia and Central Asia*, New Delhi: Publications Division, Government of India, 1973.

Saberwal, V.K. 1999. Pastoral politics: shepherds, bureaucrats, and conservation in the Western Himalaya (Studies in Social Ecology and Environmental History), New York: Oxford University Press.

The *Saṃyutta Nikāya Aṭṭhakathā*, ed. F.L. Woodward, *the Sāratthappakāsinī*, Buddhaghosa's commentary on the *Saṃyutta Nikāya*, 3 vols, London: PTS, 1977.

Sankrityayan, R. 1948. *Kinnara Deśa Meṅ*, 3rd ed, New Delhi: Kitab Mahal Agencies, 1990 (originally published, 1948).

Sherring, Charles A. 1906. *Western Tibet and the Indian Borderland*, First Indian Edition, Delhi: Cosmo Publications, 1974 (originally published, 1906).

Singh, S.P. 1995. "Origin and Growth of the Institution of Pilgrimage," in D.P. Dubey (ed), *Pilgrimage Studies: Sacred Places Sacred Traditions*, Allahabad: The Society of Pilgrimage Studies: 9ff.

Skorupski T. (ed). 1990. *Indo-Tibetan Studies: papers in Honour and Appreciation of Professor David L. Snellgrove's Contribution to Indo-Tibetan Studies*, Buddhica Britannica Series Continua 11, Tring: Institute of Buddhist Studies.

Snellgrove, D. 1981. *Himalayan Pilgrimage*, Boston: Shambala, 1989 (first published, 1981).

Snelling, J. 1990. *The Sacred Mountain: Travellers and Pilgrims at Mount Kailas in Western Tibet, and Great Universal Symbol of the Sacred Mountain*, 2nd rev ed, London: East West Publications.

Staal. F. 1990. "The Lake of the Yaksa Chief," in T. Skorupski (ed), *Indo-Tibetan Studies: papers in Honour and Appreciation of Professor David L. Snellgrove's Contribution to Indo-Tibetan Studies*, Buddhica Britannica Series Continua 11, Tring: Institute of Buddhist Studies, 1990: 275-292.

Stevenson, M.S. 1999. *Heart of Jainism*, New Delhi: Munshiram Manoharlal.

Strachey, H. 1848. *Narrative of a Journey to the Lakes Cho Lagan or Rakas Tal, and Cho Mapan, or Manasarowar*, Calcutta: Baptist Mission Press.

The Sutta-Nipāta Aṭṭhakathā, ed. H. Smith, *Sutta-Nipāta commentary being Paramatthajotikā II*, 3 vols, London: PTS, 1916-18.

Teasdill, Wendy. 1998. *Walking to the Mountain: A Pilgrimage to Tibet's Holy Mount Kailash*, Hong Kong: Asia 2000.

Teichman, E. 1922. *Travels of a Consular Officer in Eastern Tibet; together with a History of the relations between China, Tibet and India*, Cambridge: Cambridge University Press.

Thapar, R. 1981. "The Householder and the Renouncer in the Brahmanical and Buddhist Traditions," in Madan T.N. (ed). *Way of Life: King, Householder, Renouncer, Studies in Honour of Louis Dumont*, New Delhi: Vikas.

Thapar, R. 1978. "Renunciation: The Making of a Counter-Culture?," in R. Thapar (ed), *Ancient Indian Social History: Some Interpretations*, New Delhi: Orient Longman.

The Theragāthā Aṭṭhakathā, ed. F.L. Woodward, *Paramattha-Dīpanī: Theragāthā-Aṭṭhakathā, The Commentary of Dhammapālācariya*, 3 vols, London: PTS, 1940-59 (mentioned as ThA in the notes).

Thorpe, B. (ed). 1849, *Ancient Laws and Institutes of England*, London: George E. Eyre & Andrew Spottiswoode.

Trenckner, V. (tr). 1880. *Milindapañha*, London: Williams and Norgate: 1880.

Tucci, G. 1937. *Sadhus et brigands du kailash: Mon voyage au Tibet occidental*, Paris: Editions Raymond Chabaud, 1989 (originally published, 1937).

Turner, V. "The Center Out There: Pilgrims' Goal," *History of Religions*, 12, 1973.

The *Udāna*, the *Theragāthā*, the *Therīgāthā*, the *Cariyāpiṭaka*, the *Itivuttaka*, the *Vimānavatthu*, and the *Petavatthu Aṭṭhakathā*, eds. F.L. Woodward, E. Hardy, E. Muller, D.L. Barua *et al*, *Paramatthadīpanī*, Dhammapālācariya's commentary on *the Udāna*, *the Theragāthā*, *the Therīgāthā*, the *Cariyāpiṭaka*, *the Itivuttaka*, *the Vimānavatthu*, and *the Petavatthu*, London: PTS, 1891-1977; Tr. W. Pruitt, *The Commentary on the Verses of the Therīs*, Oxford: PTS, 1998; P. Masefield, *The Udāna Commentary*, vol.1, Oxford: PTS, 1994.

Valli, Eric and Diane Summers. 1995. *Caravans of the Himalaya*, National Geographic Society.

Various authors. 1960. *Tibet and the People's Republic of China*, Geneva: Commission Internationale de Juristes.

Varma, R. 1988-89. *Meru and Kailasa: Reflections on a Tangible "Sacred Space"*, unpublished MA thesis, London University: SOAS.

The *Vibhaṅga Aṭṭhakathā*, ed. A.P. Buddhadatta, the *Sammohavinodanī*, London: PTS, 1923.

The *Vinaya Piṭakaṃ*, ed. H. Olderberg, 5 vols. London: PTS, 1879-1883. Translated references are from tr. I.B. Horner; *The Book of the Discipline*, 6 vols. London: PTS, 1938-1966.

The *Visuddhimagga*, ed. H.C. Warren and rev. D. Kosambi, *The Visuddhimagga of Buddhaghosācāriya*, Cambridge, Mass: Harvard Oriental Series, vol. 41, 1951.Tr. Pe Maung Tin, *The Path of Purity, being a Translation of Buddhaghosa's Visuddhimagga*, 3 vols, London, 1922-31. Tr. Bhikkhu Ñāṇamoli, *The Path of Purification (Visuddhimagga)*, Colombo, 1956.

Index